D0152217

SAVING THE MEDIA

SAVING THE MEDIA

*Capitalism, Crowdfunding,
and Democracy*

JULIA CAGÉ

Translated by

ARTHUR GOLDHAMMER

THE BELKNAP PRESS OF
HARVARD UNIVERSITY PRESS

*Cambridge, Massachusetts
London, England
2016*

First published as *Sauver les médias:*
Capitalisme, financement participatif et démocratie
© Éditions du Seuil et La République des Idées, 2015

Printed in the United States of America

First printing

Library of Congress Cataloging-in-Publication Data

Names: Cagé, Julia, author. | Goldhammer, Arthur, translator.
Title: Saving the media : capitalism, crowdfunding, and
democracy / Julia Cage ; translated by Arthur Goldhammer.
Other titles: Sauver les médias. English
Description: Cambridge, Massachusetts : The Belknap Press of
Harvard University Press, 2016. | "First published as Sauver les
medias: capitalisme, financement participatif et democratie
(c) Editions du Seuil et La Republique des Idees, 2015"—Title
page verso. | Includes bibliographical references and index.
Identifiers: LCCN 2015034378 | ISBN 9780674659759
(cloth : alk. paper)
Subjects: LCSH: Mass media—Economic aspects.
Classification: LCC P96.E25 C3413 2016 | DDC
338.4/730223—dc23 LC record available at
http://lccn.loc.gov/2015034378

CONTENTS

INTRODUCTION
For a New Form of Governance 1

Lost Illusions 3
The Media Are Not a Commodity 6
Media and Democracy 8
Saving the Media 10

1. THE INFORMATION AGE? 12

Information beyond the Media 13
Diversity of Legal Forms and Financing
    Arrangements 17
What Is News? 19
Journalists and Press Credentials 21
The Changing Size of the Journalistic Work Force 22
A Revolution in Journalism 25
Fewer and Fewer Journalists . . . per Paper 28
From Print to Web 30
Has Quality Content Decreased? 34
Has Online Content Increased? 37

CONTENTS

2. THE END OF ILLUSIONS 41

The Birth of Ad-Supported Media 42
The Illusion of Ad-Supported Media 45
Less and Less Advertising 48
The Illusion of Competition 53
The Limits of Competition 55
The Perverse Effects of Competition 61
The Illusion of Vast Internet Audiences 64
The Illusion of Subsidized Media 70
The True Importance of Press Subsidies 72
Subsidies in Context 74
Reforming Subsidies to the Press 78
The Illusion of a New Golden Age 80
The Death of One Kind of Freedom 82

3. A NEW MODEL FOR THE TWENTY-FIRST CENTURY 89

Transcending the Laws of the Market 90
The Market 94
Nonprofit Media Organizations 95
Governance and Stock 99
Existing Nonprofit Media Organizations 101
The Price of Independence 106
Limits 108
Cooperatives 110
A New Model: The NMO 114
Capital and Power 118
Voting Rights in NMOs 120

CONTENTS

Illustration   122
The Advantages of the NMO Model   125
An Alternative to Press Subsidies   129

CONCLUSION
Capitalism and Democracy   131

Replacing the Stagecoach   131
Endgame?   133

NOTES   139

INDEX   155

SAVING THE MEDIA

INTRODUCTION

For a New Form of Governance

1984. **BITS OF TORN** paper spiral in gusts of wind. What's the use of hanging on to old newspaper clippings when endless quantities of statistics can be viewed on the telescreen? In George Orwell's nightmare vision of the future, the promise of a new era of information—with screens providing news around the clock like today's cable networks—stands in stark contrast to the dark threat of disinformation. Indeed, the hero, a "journalist," is employed in faking old issues of the *Times* in order to make sure that the past corresponds to the new "reality."

2015. Screens have invaded our lives, and we communicate in Newspeak on Twitter and Facebook and in text messages and Snapchats. In the age of digital journalism, smartphones, and social networks, information is everywhere. It stares us in the face.

There have never been as many information producers as there are today. France counts more than 4,000 print newspapers and magazines; nearly 1,000 radio stations; several hundred television stations; and tens of thousands of blogs, Twitter accounts, and news aggregators. In the United States, there are nearly 1,000 local television stations, more than 15,000 radio stations, and roughly 1,300 daily papers.

Paradoxically, the media have never been in worse shape. The gross annual revenue of all daily newspapers in the United States is half that of Google, whose business model is based on winnowing content produced by others. Every "news item" is repeated ad infinitum, often without modification. Leaving aside twenty-four-hour cable news channels, which broadcast the same images over and over again in endless loops, newspapers expend more and more energy racing to publish agency dispatches on their websites, as if a quick finger on the copy-and-paste button were more important than gathering the news in the first place. Meanwhile, they regularly trim staff in their press rooms. The media production system simply cannot tolerate unlimited competition among ever-increasing numbers of players.

In the world of the media, these are the best of times and the worst of times. There is some reason for optimism: never have there been so many newspaper readers. The readership numbers are dazzling—so much so that certain sites (mainly blogs) pay their "contributors" on the basis of traffic generated.

Yet the statistics showing tens of millions of Internet viewers are highly misleading. The underlying reality is far less hopeful. Although newspapers are reaching growing numbers of readers through online sites, they have been unable to "monetize" their new digital audience. Indeed, in chasing the online ad revenue on which they are convinced their future depends, newspapers have sacrificed the quality they need to keep up their print circulation without generating sufficient compensatory income from their online presence. They are slowly sinking, awaiting their ultimate demise.

Lost Illusions

The media are experiencing a serious crisis. It would be easy to multiply examples of print media laying off workers and newspapers going out of business around the world. In 2012 France lost two national dailies, *France-Soir* and *La Tribune*. In 2014 the Nice-Matin Group, which ended 2013 with an operating loss of 6 million euros, was placed in receivership. The newspaper *Libération,* which narrowly avoided bankruptcy, laid off a third of its employees at the beginning of 2015 while *Le Figaro* organized "voluntary departures" and *Sud-Ouest* cut its staff sharply. In Germany more than 1,000 media jobs disappeared in 2013, and in Spain some 200 media outlets vanished between 2008 and 2012. Things were little better in the United States. The website Newspaper Death Watch mourns the disappearance of twelve local dailies since 2007 and notes an equal number "on the way out," leaving many markets without a daily paper.[1] Although the *Chicago Tribune* and the *Los Angeles Times* continue to publish, both declared bankruptcy in 2008, a year in which American newspapers shed more than 15,000 jobs.[2]

The crisis has affected more than just the print media. In late 2013 France Televisions (the French public national television broadcaster) proposed a voluntary departure plan affecting 361 jobs while in early 2015 Radio France (the public service radio broadcaster) experienced the longest strike in its history as the government slashed its budget and began withdrawing financial support. In the United Kingdom, the British Broadcasting Corporation (BBC) announced in 2014 that it would eliminate 220 jobs in its news division by 2016 under a plan dubbed

"Delivering Quality First," designed to give "priority to quality broadcasting." British humor. Then it announced that 1,000 jobs would be cut in July 2015 owing to a decrease in revenue from the license fee that finances the public broadcasting service in Britain—icing on a cake that was becoming more indigestible by the hour.

One crucial fact: there is nothing new about this crisis. It did not begin with the advent of the Internet or the financial collapse of 2008. We tend to forget that with each new technological innovation—radio, television, the Internet—the print media and their newer competitors have howled at the intensification of competition, which they were certain meant impending death. Even in the United States, where advertising is king, newspaper ad revenue has been declining as a percentage of gross domestic product (GDP) since 1956.

Still, the crisis has grown radically worse in recent years. The traditional media are under siege, with their backs to the wall. News is borrowed, relayed, and duplicated without compensation, even though it is costly to produce. More news than ever pours from the cornucopia, but the media themselves are on their last legs. Consider this historical irony: Émile de Girardin, who created the penny press in France and is often touted as one of the first media entrepreneurs, began his career in 1828 with *Le Voleur (The Thief)*, a weekly that filled its pages with the best items of the week stolen from other publications.

The Media Are Not a Commodity

Citizens, whether aware of these developments or not, are increasingly distrustful of the traditional media. In France, although interest in the news remains high, less than a quarter of people surveyed say they trust the media. According to a 2014 Gallup poll, only 22 percent of Americans trust their newspapers, only 19 percent trust the Internet, and only 18 percent trust televised news. Why such suspicion?

This wariness of newspapers, journalists, and press barons is by no means new. In the late nineteenth century, scandals relating to the financing of the Panama Canal and Russian railroads revealed the corruption of some French newspapers. American newspapers also became the butt of criticism in this period. Throughout the nineteenth century, politicians used newspapers as public relations tools, and few were truly independent.[3] Nevertheless, today's levels of distrust are worrisome, both in absolute terms and in relation to the ideal of information transparency that the new technologies should, in principle, make possible—to say nothing of the democratic hopes to which the twentieth century gave rise.

In the aftermath of World War II, efforts were made to give the press a special legal status. Good intentions were plentiful, and speech after speech repeated them, but the press remained subject to the laws governing private enterprise. Most newspapers were owned by their stockholders and subject to the laws of the market. They could be bought, sold, and even stripped of their assets.

France-Soir, a leading French paper until the early 1970s, fell into the hands of the Hersant Group, ceased to pay its suppliers, was bought out, suffered a strike by its workers that kept it off the newsstands for more than a month, changed its format and editor, and then in 2010 was acquired by the Russian billionaire Alexander Pugachev, who quickly tired of it. In the United States, dozens of newspapers have changed hands in recent years: the investment bank Dirks, Van Essen & Murray catalogued seventy-one sales of newspapers in 2011 alone while in 2012 Media General Inc. sold all of its newspaper properties. These and countless other examples demonstrate how capitalists control the media, which they regard as assets like any other. In many cases the structure of ownership is far from transparent. Similarly, local television stations in the United States have in recent years been bought and sold with unprecedented frequency.

Nevertheless, the media in the United States, the United Kingdom, Germany, and Italy have often been innovative in their response. Nonprofit journalism has grown far more rapidly in these countries than in France. Some media outlets, such as the *Guardian* in Britain, are owned by foundations; the Bertelsmann Foundation plays a similar role in Germany. The American billionaires Herbert and Marion Sandler founded the nonprofit ProPublica in 2008. Of course, Herbert Sandler serves as chair of the ProPublica board, which shows that even in the world of nonprofits, power resides where the money is.

Media and Democracy

With this we come to the heart of the challenge that this book will take up: to propose a new model of governance and financing that will allow the news media to avoid the dangers that threaten them.

First, the media have all too often served as toys for billionaires in search of influence. In what kind of democracy are we living when we must rejoice that a real-estate speculator and a mobile-telephone magnate turned up just in the nick of time to "save" *Libération*? Must we loudly applaud a new golden age in American media because a number of billionaires have generously reached into their pockets to save venerable old newspapers?

Just as genuine democracy cannot survive if political life is financed by a few individuals with unlimited resources, we cannot have the media on which the quality of democratic debate depends beholden solely to billionaires with bottomless pockets. Not only do we need a diversity of newspapers and television networks; we also need a *diversity in the ownership of the media*. We must have diverse multiple stockholders in order to ensure that the majority of voting rights is not held by a minority of investors.

Second, experience teaches us that when a media outlet is owned solely by its employees (as was the case, for example, with the Sociétés Coopératives Ouvrières de Production, or Workers' Production Cooperatives, in France and elsewhere), failure is inevitable. The idea of self-managed journalism is utopian if one sticks to the strict principle of "one worker, one vote."

Other formulas such as the societies of readers or journalists—in which readers and journalists themselves are stockholders of the newspaper—are no panacea either.[4] Consider the case of *Le Monde,* which teaches us that conflicts between a nominal stakeholder with decreasing equity capital, such as *Le Monde*'s Society of Journalists, and the investors who hold the actual majority of voting rights can prove fatal unless a previously agreed-upon resolution procedure is in place. What is needed is an innovative solution adapted to today's realities: a new form of ownership participation with shared control of rights and decision-making power or, in other words, a new form of stockholder democracy adapted to the media and perhaps to other enterprises as well.

Saving the Media

To transcend the contradictions enumerated above, this book presents a *new corporate model for the media,* a model adapted to the twenty-first century. It proposes a new type of entity, a *nonprofit media organization,* intermediate in status between a foundation and a corporation. This model is inspired in part by successful experiments in the media sector in recent years, as well as by major universities that combine commercial and nonprofit activities in a single entity.

With this ambitious model, it is possible to provide media actors with secure capital while imposing statutory constraints on the power of outside stock-holders. It provides a new place for societies of readers and employees as well as a legal and fiscal framework suitable for crowdfunding (participatory financing). It also simplifies the provision of government aid to the media compared with the complex system in place in France today.[5] Finally, in a country like the United States, where the government plays a much smaller role in financing the media than in France, the new model provides an efficient way to increase state investment in this area.

The new model can guarantee the quality of the media by ensuring a stable provision of capital through long-term investments. No longer will the media be a playground for entrepreneurs in search of entertainment nor a hunting ground for speculators in search of lucrative deals. By reducing the decision-making power of the largest stockholders and placing significant countervailing power in the hands of readers, listeners, and viewers as well as journalists, this model is aimed at democratic reappropriation of the media by those who produce and consume the news rather than by those who seek to shape public opinion or to use their money to influence our votes and our decisions.

· 1 ·

THE INFORMATION AGE?

ARE WE LIVING in an information society? Is the number of journalists and, more broadly, content producers increasing steadily or shrinking dramatically? Is the quality of information improving, or have we simply been inundated with a flood of low-quality news?

Before considering ways of resolving the current crisis of the media, we need an accurate diagnosis of the situation. We need a better understanding of who produces the news, how it is transmitted, and who consumes it. And we need to look not only at information provided by the media but more generally at knowledge conveyed by cultural industries, universities, museums, theater, and film. In other words, our subject is information as a public good, an essential ingredient of political participation in a democracy.

Although information is a public good, it resembles many other cultural goods in that the state cannot produce it directly. Rethinking the economic model of the media must take place at the crossroads where state and market, public sector and private sector, intersect. The problems of the media are problems of today's *knowledge economy*—and so are the solutions. The knowledge- and culture-producing sectors long ago developed models that sidestep the laws of the market without succumbing to state control. By drawing on these models, the media can create new options for themselves and resolve the crisis.

Information beyond the Media

It is difficult to estimate precisely how much the knowledge sector contributes to the economy. In addition to the cultural sector, higher education and research also contribute.

According to a recent official report, "culture" in the strict sense accounts for 3.2 percent of French GDP, seven times as much as the automobile industry and the equivalent of the agricultural and food sectors combined.[1] Directly or indirectly, the cultural sector employs 670,000 people, or 2.5 percent of total employment. For the purposes of this discussion, culture includes the periodical press, book publishing, audiovisual production, advertising, theater and other productions before a live audience, historic monuments and heritage sites, visual arts, architecture, film, "sound and image industries," and institutions providing "access to knowledge and culture." Similarly, artistic and cultural production accounts for 3.2 percent of US GDP, which is more than the travel and tourist industries combined (2.8 percent).[2] In the United Kingdom, so-called creative industries represent an estimated 5.2 percent of GDP.[3]

But that is not the whole story. Institutions of higher education and research play a central role in the production and transmission of knowledge, often in symbiosis with the cultural sectors and the media, which they far outweigh in terms of share of GDP. Higher education and research currently account for 3.8 percent of French GDP (1.5 percent for higher education and a little less than 2.3 percent for research) and 5.6 percent of US GDP (2.8 percent for higher education and another 2.8 for research).[4] As for employment, higher education and research employ 650,000 people in France, accounting for nearly 2.5 percent of total employment. Jobs in public and private research organizations (including research and development) number 400,000 (of which 250,000 are in research) while 150,000 are employed in public and private higher education (including roughly 80,000 instructors and researchers).

Thus, if we combine culture, higher education, and research, we find that the sector accounts for nearly 7 percent of French GDP and nearly 5 percent of employment. If we add primary and secondary education, we easily exceed 10 percent of GDP, which can be broken down roughly into thirds: one-third for culture, one-third for higher education, and one-third for primary and secondary education. The orders of magnitude are similar in the United States, with an even greater share for higher education and research.

The media make up a relatively small proportion of this very significant sector. The print media, radio, and television contribute somewhat less than 30 percent of the total for the knowledge sector. In France there are nearly twice as many teachers and researchers as journalists (and in the United States close to three times as many), and if current trends continue, this ratio will increase. Between 1992 and 2013, the number of teachers and researchers grew by 67 percent while the number of journalists increased only by 38 percent (unevenly distributed across the various media).

Yet the media sector remains significant because of the size of its audience. Higher education in France serves some 2.4 million students, or roughly a third of the number of readers of the local daily press. Even if we look at the educational system as a whole, the total number of students and apprentices in France (15.2 million) is only slightly larger than the combined viewership of news broadcasts on the TF1, France 2, Arte, and M6 networks (13.6 million). Musical theater in France attracts 1.4 million spectators to 1,000 shows every season, less than one-sixth the number of monthly unique visitors to *Le Monde*'s website. The Opéra National de Paris entertains 328,000 spectators with its ballets annually, less than the average daily readership of just one local newspaper, *Ouest-France*.

One hears frequent—and justified—complaints about declining interest in the print media. Yet while more than two-thirds of French people above the age of fifteen regularly read a daily newspaper, fewer than 60 percent go to the movies at least once a year, barely a third visit a museum or an art gallery, and only a fifth go to the theater. The picture is similar elsewhere in Europe and in the United States.

This is the paradox of the media and in particular the press. A small number of organizations, accounting for a relatively small proportion of the economy and employing an even smaller proportion of the work force, reach a very large portion of the public and are in a position to influence decisions crucial to the proper working of our democracies. Because universal suffrage is no longer capable of legitimating political power, democracy must rely more than ever on the countervailing power of the media.[5]

Diversity of Legal Forms and Financing Arrangements

The countervailing power of the media takes a variety of forms. In France most newspapers are joint-stock companies, but more than two-thirds of radio stations are nonprofit organizations. Firms in the broader knowledge economy come in a variety of legal forms. Although some of the largest international media firms (such as the New York Times Company) are listed on stock exchanges, virtually no universities are. (Some colleges and universities in the United States that attempted to operate as for-profit corporations failed spectacularly—the most striking example being Corinthian Colleges Inc.—while others made headlines for their poor performance. Today, it seems highly unlikely that this model will spread, all the more so because Obama's recent 90/10 proposal threatens the viability of several for-profit institutions.)[6]

The world's greatest universities, with capital endowments exceeding $30 billion in the case of Harvard, Yale, and Princeton, have more equity than the largest banks, yet they are organized as non-profit foundations, and no one would think of transforming them into joint-stock companies. Public money plays a substantial role in financing universities in all countries, including the United States, supplementing income from research contracts and tuition fees. Yet this dependence on public funding does not compromise the independence of these institutions. Think tanks, theaters, cinemas, production studios, and primary and secondary schools exist in a variety of legal forms with different modes of governance, financing arrangements, and power structures.

The stockholder model has not proved up to the challenges facing the media today. In an increasingly competitive environment, media companies have been driven to cut costs and in particular to cut staff, when it would have been preferable to secure permanent financing and bet on quality. The media have tended to abandon news in favor of "infotainment" or just plain entertainment, which is far less costly to produce and often more remunerative in terms of advertising revenue, leaving growing numbers of people without access to high-quality information.

The point is not to pass judgment on the value of this or that television program or to distinguish between serious newspaper articles and merely entertaining ones. News is not intrinsically "superior" to entertainment. But just as we believe that schools should provide everyone with access to a minimum level of knowledge and competence, we hold that information is a public good that should be *accessible to everyone*. Because access to the news should be protected, we need to rethink the way news is produced in today's environment.

What Is News?

Let us dwell for a moment on the notion of news as a public good produced by journalists. What is it? Are we talking about articles published in so-called general interest newspapers and posted on their websites?

Or items posted on the sites of so-called pure players, that is, news outlets without a corresponding print edition? Or televised news? Or exclusive radio interviews? Or blog posts? Or simple tweets? Or photos posted on Instagram or videos on YouTube? Are all of these things news? Or none of them?

Everyone agrees that an article published in the *New York Times* about conflicts on the Syrian border between al-Qaeda and the Islamic State is news. It is less clear that the birth of a royal baby is news, although the media seem to have decided that it is. If a first lady tweets a Valentine's Day love note, is that news? By what stroke of the magic wand is a simple tweet transformed into news? Here, news agencies play a fundamental role. The function of a news agency is to provide rapid, accurate, and complete information. Rumor, gossip, and buzz become news the instant they are reported in an agency dispatch, which can then be repeated and dissected by other media.

In France the legal definition of news is important because it establishes the right to certain public subsidies. Under the law, news is original content "related to current events and subject to treatment of a journalistic character." Hence it is journalistic labor that turns mere "fact" into news. In short, news is defined by defining its producers: journalists. In the digital age, where news is transmitted in real time via blogs and social networks, it is sometimes said that every web surfer is a journalist, but this is incorrect. Journalism is a profession.

Journalists and Press Credentials

What distinguishes a real journalist from a Sunday blogger? In France it is basically the possession of a press card. Since 1936 press cards valid for a period of one year have been issued by the Commission on Professional Journalist Identity Cards (CCIJP). To be considered a journalist under the law, one must have a press card, which clears the way for accreditation at public events and entitles the journalist to certain tax deductions.

Under the French labor code, a professional journalist is "any person whose primary, regular, and remunerated professional activity is associated with one or more daily or periodical publications or news agencies, which provide essential resources." This tautological definition begs to be improved. According to the charter of journalistic ethics issued by France's National Journalists Union (SNJ), "Journalism consists in researching, fact-checking, contextualizing, structuring, editing, commenting, and publishing high-quality information."

The Changing Size of the Journalistic Work Force

In France nearly 37,000 press cards were issued in 2013. Is that a large number or a small one? It represents just under 0.14 percent of the active population. For comparison, there are nearly 170,000 journalists in the United States, or 0.12 percent of the active population, and 70,000 in Germany, or almost 0.18 percent. The orders of magnitude are similar, so it is reasonable to ask about the long-term evolution of the profession.

The number of journalists in France, both in absolute terms and as a percentage of the active population, increased sharply after World War II, rising to 35,000 in 2000, and then leveled off. Since then, occasional slight increases in the number of card-carrying journalists have alternated with significant decreases (see Figure 1).

Does the long-term increase in the number of journalists suggest a growing influence of the news media in contemporary society? Or does it reflect the increased presence of the "intellectual professions" in

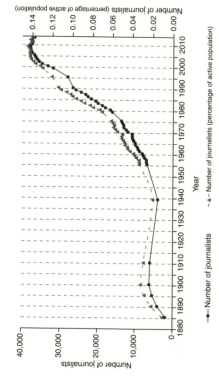

FIGURE 1. Number of journalists in France, 1880–2013

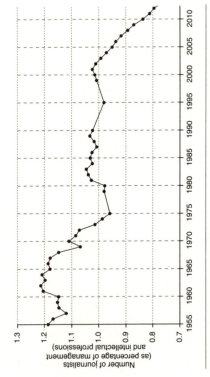

FIGURE 2. Number of journalists as a percentage of total employment in management and higher intellectual professions, France, 1955–2013

general? It is striking that the proportion of journalists among workers classified as "management and higher intellectual professions" has actually decreased since 1965 (see Figure 2).[7]

In other words, when we take the growing complexity of society into account, we find that journalists today are proportionately fewer in number than they were fifty years ago. Yet as society grows more complex, journalists' insights are arguably more necessary than ever. Indeed, part of the work of the journalist consists in making the broader public aware of what other knowledge workers are producing. If there are fewer journalists around to do this work, who will take their place?

In any case, these fluctuations in the number of journalists should not be allowed to conceal an important change in the nature of the profession, namely, the fact that fewer and fewer journalists are employed by newspapers.

A Revolution in Journalism

In France today 66 percent of journalists work for the print media; in 1964 more than 90 percent did. Fewer than 22 percent work for the daily (regional and national) general-interest press, sharply down from the

1960s, when the figure was above 50 percent. Even more striking is the fact that within the print media the range of activities in which journalists are engaged has widened enormously. Growing numbers of those employed by print media organizations are assigned to web support tasks, yet the growth of the Internet does not seem to have slowed the decrease in the total number of journalists. French dailies have shed nearly 1,000 jobs since 2007.

The decrease in the number of journalists employed by the daily press is not limited to France. In the United States, the decline began in 1990, when there were 57,000 daily journalists, compared with only 38,000 today, well below the level of the late 1970s (43,000). As a percentage of the active population, the number of daily journalists has been decreasing since 1985 (see Figure 3).

Is the Internet to blame for this decrease? As the graph clearly shows, neither the financial crisis of 2008 nor the advent of the Internet can bear all the blame for the drop in journalistic employment. Other factors were also at work. Admittedly, the crisis of the print media has worsened since the late 2000s. But the Internet only amplified a broader phenomenon: increased competition in the media market owing first to radio, then television, and today the web.

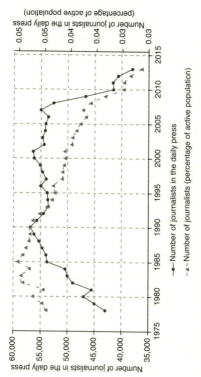

FIGURE 3. Number of journalists in the daily press in the United States, 1978–2013

This increased competition explains both the revolution in journalism—the decrease in the number of journalists working for print media as opposed to other media—and the economic crisis of the press, which has seen its advertising revenues collapse as competition has increased.

Fewer and Fewer Journalists . . . per Paper

With daily press journalists representing 0.03 percent of the active population, France finds itself in the middle of the pack of developed countries, with Japan leading and the United States and Italy trailing behind. The picture has changed a lot in the last few decades: when expressed as a percentage of the active population, the number of daily press journalists in the United States has been cut by half since 1980.

These numbers conceal the degree to which individual newspapers have been affected, because the decrease in the total number of journalists cannot be attributed solely to the failure of many publications. Surviving papers have also cut their staffs. In Spain, *El Pais* laid off 129 of its 440 journalists in 2012. In the United States, in 2013 alone the *Cleveland Plain Dealer* eliminated fifty jobs and the *Portland Oregonian* thirty-five while the Gannett group laid off 400 and the Tribune Company trimmed nearly 700 jobs from its payroll. According to the annual census conducted by the American Society of News Editors, there were roughly 1,400 daily papers in the United States in 2013, employing 38,000 journalists, for an average of twenty-seven journalists per paper, compared with thirty-nine in 2001.

Why is this a problem? One might think that it makes no difference whether you have one newspaper employing 100 journalists or two newspapers employing fifty each. In both cases, 100 journalists are at work producing information. We will examine this point at greater length when we look at the limits of competition in the media sector. For now, suffice it to say that the difficulty stems from the way news organizations are structured.

Consider two general-interest papers covering political news. Even if their political orientations are different, there are certain stories that both papers must cover (on a given day, these might include fighting in Iraq, a bus accident involving students returning from summer camp, and a presidential press conference). Hence, both papers will assign people to cover these stories, and there will be duplication not only of content but also of effort. Less effort will therefore be devoted to ferreting out new stories or analyzing events in greater depth. In economic terms, the production of news is characterized by extremely high fixed costs relative to the cost of reproduction.

The purpose of news agencies is to reduce this useless duplication of effort. In the United States, newspapers joined together to create the Associated Press (AP) in order to report the news more efficiently. But this was only a partial solution because subscriptions to the agency's news wires are very expensive (although in France the Agence-France Presse [AFP] is indirectly subsidized by the state) and because media organizations must assign more and more reporters to the task of reproducing agency dispatches on an almost real-time basis for their websites.

From Print to Web

In recent years, news organizations have not only cut newsroom staffs overall but also increased the proportion of their employees assigned to web maintenance duties. It is increasingly common to distinguish young and successful "web journalists" from plain old-fashioned journalists—has-beens on the way to extinction.

At *Le Monde* in France, an internal reorganization plan (which led to the removal of the paper's managing editor in 2014) proposed moving fifty print journalists, nearly one-sixth of the staff, to web duties. In 2013 the *Daily Telegraph* in the United Kingdom laid off eighty print journalists while hiring fifty web journalists. In the United States, some 500 online news sites have hired nearly 5,000 full-time workers over the past six years, while newspaper jobs continue to disappear. Some of these new jobs were created by pure players: BuzzFeed today employs 170 journalists, Gawker 132, and Mashable 70. But the majority of new hires were with the websites of print media, which gradually shifted already-slashed resources from print to the web.

Let me be clear: this is not a plea to save the print media. I have no particular preference for ink over tablets. The print media are likely to disappear, which in itself is not a problem. Nor is it a problem that more and more people receive their news via podcast or the web rather than from television. How news is consumed matters little. France recognized in 2009 that news is defined not by a material medium—paper—but rather by editorial content, for which the Internet is a legitimate medium. What matters is the quality of the information. This is all too often forgotten.

To be sure, hiring skilled web journalists has contributed to some interesting and beneficial technological innovations, such as improved online graphics and data-driven journalism. With one click it is now possible to obtain detailed, graphically illustrated election results for any election, almost in real time. Interactive links, online videos, and animated graphics promote a better understanding of the news.

But at what cost? The digital revolution has come at a time of constrained resources so that most outlets have taken advantage of digital not as a complement to quality news (intended for print as well as the web) but as a substitute. Print journalists have been replaced by computer specialists and Java experts who are given no opportunity to leave their screens to do shoe-leather reporting. The high cost of creating websites compatible with a range of different devices has frequently been met by cutting the resources allocated to investigative reporting.

How have these staff substitutions compounded the long-term competitive crisis of the media? Newspapers have closed foreign news bureaus, laid off veteran correspondents, and cut back on local and national political coverage. An investigative journalist can cost a newspaper more than $250,000 a year in salary and expenses, in return for which it is likely to get a relatively small number of articles. According to Éric Scherer, the *Boston Globe* spent more than $1 million on an eight-month investigation that led to sexual abuse charges against members of the Catholic clergy in 2002, on top of which the paper had to absorb tens of thousands of dollars in court costs.[8]

In the United States, it has become harder and harder to find news about politics at the state level, where corruption is rampant, and local newspapers used to serve as a much-needed countervailing power. The number of foreign correspondents employed by US papers decreased by 24 percent between 2003 and 2010. Nightly network news broadcasts have cut their foreign news coverage by half since 1990.

Of course, the picture is not totally bleak. Interestingly, the pure players that have created many new jobs have also invested in international reporting. Vice Media has thirty-five foreign bureaus; the Huffington Post is present in eleven countries; and Quartz has reporters in London, Bangkok, and Hong Kong. In France, the online Mediapart has in recent years played a key role in uncovering several corruption scandals involving politicians of both the Left and Right.

Unfortunately, such sites are relatively rare. The largest of them employ no more than a hundred journalists (Mediapart has fewer than fifty), and they cannot replace the exhaustive coverage of national and international news that traditional newspapers used to provide.

Has Quality Content Decreased?

It is difficult to measure the quality of the content offered by the media or to compare the content of one outlet with that of another. It is even more complicated to measure the evolution of quality over time. Of course, one often reads that the average American city paper offered much more comprehensive national and international as well as local news coverage fifty years ago than can be found today. It is also common to hear that this or that paper "is no longer what it used to be." The fact that any number of journalistic superstars—from Jack Kelley to Bill O'Reilly, Jayson Blair, and Brian Williams—have been caught "embellishing" their reporting or their past exploits is hardly reassuring as to the quality of the news available to the general public. But it does not follow that we are less well informed today than in the past.

Objectivity is difficult to achieve, but quantitative measures can help. Consider, for example, the evolution of the number of journalists. Counting pages of newsprint provides a more direct but crude quantitative measure. Page counts in the major international dailies increased from 1950 to 1990. The rate of increase then slowed, and by 2000 page counts began to shrink for the major French dailies. Leading papers in other countries experienced similar shrinkage somewhat later.[9]

Page counts fail to capture the effect of changes in typeface, however. If we compare the March 18, 1950, edition of the *New York Times* with that of March 18, 2014—sixty-four years later—the difference is striking: not only has the amount of white space increased considerably but the font size is also much larger, and there are many more photographs where there used to be text.[10] Page counts also fail to register changes in page size. In France the size of the average newspaper or magazine page decreased by more than a third between 1965 and 2015. For instance, *La Croix*'s page size shrank from 43×60 centimeters (cm) to 29.5×42.7 cm and *Le Figaro*'s from 40.5×60 cm to 35.5×45.5 cm. Following the lead of other US papers, including the *Wall Street Journal,* the *Washington Post,* and the *Los Angeles Times,* the *New York Times* also reduced its page size in 2006, decreasing the space devoted to news by 5 percent.[11]

To be sure, it has become commonplace for newspapers and magazines to publish supplements. The

New York Times offers as many as fifteen Sunday supplements (arts and leisure, travel, sports, style, real estate, automobiles, etc.) in addition to extra sections during the week, some with ten or more additional pages. But these supplements, including *M* (*Le Monde*'s weekly magazine), the *Times Magazine* in the United Kingdom, and the *Sydney Morning Herald*'s *Good Weekend,* are also vehicles for advertising, and the content is often closer to entertainment than news.

It bears emphasizing that this quantitative decrease in output is not due to a sudden fall-off in journalistic productivity. Cuts in both staffing and resources are responsible. This is an important point. Many people (especially economists) shrug their shoulders when told of newsroom layoffs and argue that staff cuts must surely be offset by productivity gains. It's good news, they say, that each journalist can now produce more with less. Newspapers will be able to cut costs and raise profits by laying off staff. This is what technological progress is all about! Unfortunately, this argument misses the point of what is actually happening, namely, that newspapers are cutting costs *at the expense of quality.*

What we might call "the theory of productivity gains" is usually coupled with a hint of anti-French sentiment: French papers are criticized for their in-competence compared with their counterparts in the English-speaking world. Such criticism neglects the fact that the *New York Times* still employs more than 1,000 journalists, three times the staff of *Le Monde,* and it can obviously afford to do so because it serves a much larger market. If we take the entire universe of newspapers as our sample, we find that there is a very strong correlation between number of pages and number of journalists.

Of course, one can always dream about the advent of "robot journalists," which are already being used in the United States to write wedding announce-ments and stories based on corporate annual reports. But these robots are like news aggregators: they feed on information generated elsewhere and relayed by the Internet. The plain truth is this: without journal-ists, there is no news.

Has Online Content Increased?

But by concentrating on print newspapers, aren't we underestimating the actual quantity of information? Obviously, it is important to ask whether online content has made up for the decrease in newspaper page counts. Today, a great deal of news is indeed published in digital form, partly for strategic reasons, to increase the organization's web traffic, and partly for cost reasons. Publishing additional print pages increases production costs (for printing, paper, and delivery), whereas the marginal cost of publishing online is nil.

What is striking about the websites of the leading daily papers is the amount of online content derived from news agency dispatches. There is a race to be first, not with scoops, as was the case a few decades ago, but with cutting and pasting dispatches from the AP, AFP, and Reuters. Sometimes, these sites simply publish tweets with a bare minimum of commentary. The problem is not that journalists have become habituated to cut-and-paste journalism but that in a society in which information can be reproduced in real time at no cost, the incentives to do deep reporting (and to bear the necessary investigative costs) have all but disappeared.

In the United States in the nineteenth century, journalists vied to be first with the news because being the first to break a story could yield significant circulation gains. Today's news organizations must publish every dispatch, sometimes without editing, lest the reader click on another site and disappear. Google News acts as editor-in-chief for newspaper websites. And those sites, in addition to relaying agency dispatches in real time, often republish the same stories with a slight change of headline or lead in order to increase their click and link counts.[12]

Remember, too, that the Internet, like radio and television before it, depends heavily on the print media. In a humorous vein, the novelist Mario Vargas Llosa has written about how the news bulletins broadcast by Peru's Radio Panamericana in the 1950s were in fact based on articles published in *El Comercio* and *La Prensa* and rewritten by the fictional hero Varguitas, pompously dubbed the station's "news director."[13] In France it is commonplace to say that the anchors on the nightly network news are reading from copies of *Le Monde* spread out on their laps. Even Eric Schmidt, the former chief executive officer (CEO) of Google, admits that Google "desperately needs newspapers, magazines, and news organizations to succeed, because we need content."[14]

Some news aggregators practice their own brand of journalism. In 2013, for example, Yahoo News hired several journalists who had previously worked for the *New York Times* to produce original content. Today, Yahoo News employs fifty journalists. Pure players such as Mediapart and Politico produce news online just as they would for print. Nevertheless, 80 percent of the links on US news sites, blogs, and social networks refer to traditional media.

Some observers argue that the media themselves are responsible for this worrisome situation because of their many mistakes and their failure to adapt to the new world in which they find themselves. My diagnosis is somewhat different: the media have not hit on the right economic model because they have failed to comprehend the nature of the crisis and therefore continue to react with outdated reflexes.

· 2 ·

THE END OF ILLUSIONS

THE NEWS IS in danger. The web and the expectation that news should be available for free threaten the viability not only of print media but also of radio and television. Journalists are disappearing, and without them there is no news. Yet nothing is being done. Why such passivity?

The crisis of the media is far from invisible. It is often front-page news. But its causes are not well understood. Most debate is focused on "the death of print," but what matters is not the medium but the message. There is also some discussion of how to charge for digital access. Should news be paid for by the item? Can free access be combined with paid access? Should websites establish paywalls? These are no doubt important questions, but so much attention has been devoted to them that the more important issues of quality content and the organizational structure of the media have been neglected.

What is striking is the sheer amount of energy devoted to inventing "innovative" pay schemes to extract additional revenue from advertising. This will never work, and existing ad revenue is destined to dry up. The advertising illusion is the first of four illusions that keeps journalists, media owners, politicians, and the public from proposing any useful solution to the crisis. The other three are the illusion of competition, the illusion of subsidized media, and the illusion of a new golden age.

The Birth of Ad-Supported Media

The media are "subject to influence." The media are "commodities." Some argue that the greatest danger the media face is pressure from advertisers. In their view, newspapers and other media organizations are entirely at the mercy of advertisers, to whom they are prepared to sell "brain share" and alter their coverage of certain issues. To do otherwise is to risk losing the revenue they need to meet expenses.[1]

In contrast, others say that advertising guarantees the independence of the media and that the only way to resolve the crisis is to capture new ad revenue. Without money from advertising, they argue, a new age of corruption is inevitable. Yet the truth is that advertising revenue is dwindling. This is a long-term development not likely to be reversed. Still, the issue of editorial independence from the influence of advertisers remains significant because as ad revenue disappears, the media must compete even harder for what little remains. Recent events may serve as a reminder: in early 2015 Peter Oborne resigned, with much fanfare, from the *Daily Telegraph* to protest the paper's failure to cover the SwissLeaks scandal in order to avoid offending the bank HSBC, one of its primary advertisers.

For many years advertising money kept newspapers financially afloat and afforded them a degree of independence vis-à-vis governments in both Europe and the United States. The *Times* of London was born in 1788 when an advertising bulletin named the *Daily Universal Register* was transformed into a daily newspaper. By 1800 this quality daily was publishing ads on its front page, from which it derived the revenue necessary to keep publishing. In France, newspaper advertising appeared somewhat later in response to a political decision. A law of March 15, 1827, increased postal fees on newspapers by 150 percent. The price was based not on the weight but on the number of pages. Hence, publishers chose to move to larger formats and to open their pages to ads, which brought in new revenue to make up for the increased costs of paper and postage.[2]

Above all, advertising allowed newspapers to cut prices and to increase circulation. In France, Émile de Girardin is usually portrayed as the man who invented the economic model of the modern media: low cost (an annual subscription to his daily cost forty francs versus eighty for the other Parisian political dailies) compensated by substantial revenue from advertising.

In the United States, the first mass-circulation dailies appeared at about the same time and relied even more heavily on advertising revenue. The first "penny paper," the *New York Sun,* began publishing in 1833 and in just a few months outsold all other New York newspapers.[3] In 1830 the United States had only sixty-five daily newspapers with an average circulation of 1,200 (for a total of 78,000 a day), but ten years later the number had risen to 138 with an average circulation of 2,200 (for a total of 300,000). The success of the penny papers depended on the mass circulation made possible by their very low price as well as on the advertising revenue they generated.

Contemporaries spoke of the golden age of the American newspaper because advertising made papers independent of the patronage of political parties and wealthy manufacturers. Previously character-ized as "corrupt," they could now afford to be more "objective."

Is it true, then, that advertising guarantees freedom of the press? The media have long harbored this illu-sion, especially in the English-speaking world. The problem today is that the media can no longer live on their advertising revenue.

The Illusion of Ad-Supported Media

For a long time, people believed the ad market would continue to expand without limit. In most developed countries, growth in this market has slowed con-siderably in recent years, however. Figure 4 shows the total expenditure since 1980 on advertising in all media—newspapers, television, radio, Internet, the-ater, outdoor (billboards, bus shelters, . . .), etc.—as a percentage of GDP for Germany, the United States, and France.[4] Although Americans—who still spend more than 0.9 percent of GDP on advertising, more than any other developed country—remain the mas-ters of "rattling . . . a stick inside a swill-bucket" (to borrow George Orwell's definition of advertising), the fat years on Madison Avenue seem to have come to an end.

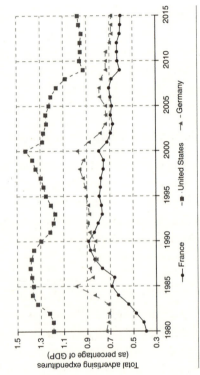

FIGURE 4. Advertising expenditures in Germany, the United States, and France, 1980–2015

American advertising expenditures have been declining as a percentage of GDP since the year 2000. Indeed, since that time they have never regained the level they achieved in 1987. In twenty years, spending on advertising decreased by 0.5 percent of GDP. Since 2010 the decline seems to have slowed, but there is no reason to think it will ever reverse.

In France and Germany, advertising expenditure has always been somewhat lower than in the United States: it never exceeded 0.9 percent of GDP in France and remains comparatively low in Germany. Yet we still find the same downward trend as in the United States. In France, after a significant increase between 1980 and 1990 (when advertising expenditure nearly doubled—but from a relatively low base by world standards), we see a steady decline of 0.3 percent of GDP. In Germany, the decrease has accelerated since 2000, and ad revenue peaked thirty years ago, in 1985. Similar decreases can be seen around the world.[5]

Several factors explain the decline of total ad expenditures. First, as new technologies have emerged, *direct marketing* has come into its own as a competitor to more traditional and less efficient forms of advertising. Second, and more important, the supply of available ad space has increased far more rapidly than the demand, owing mainly to advertising on social media such as Twitter and Facebook, so the price has dropped precipitously. The media are devoting more and more space to advertising, but it is earning them less and less.

Faced with these threats, the media have introduced some radical innovations—radical and dangerous for journalistic ethics. One such is so-called native advertising, in which ad content is made part of the normal user experience (as with sponsored links on Google). The idea is to make the user think that the ad content is part of the editorial content. I will say more about this later.

Less and Less Advertising

Thus, not only has the advertising windfall decreased, but the media's share of total advertising expenditure has also been declining for quite some time. Like the crisis of the media, the end of advertising did not begin with the advent of the Internet. Newspapers felt a shock first from competition with radio and second from competition with television.

In France, television did not carry ads until 1968, long after television advertising was introduced in other developed countries (1941 in the United States, 1955 in the United Kingdom, 1956 in Germany, and the following year in Spain and Italy).[6] This development ment drew strong protests from the press, which saw it as yet another attempt by the Gaullist government to tighten its control of the media by undermining newspapers. In fact, whatever the true motives of Prime Minister Georges Pompidou's government may have been, 1968 marks the beginning of a long decline in the share of advertising revenue going to the print media. The national dailies were the first affected, but other newspapers soon felt the shock as well.[7]

As a result, newspaper ad revenue plummeted—and not just in France. In the United States, newspaper ad revenue has been declining steadily as a percentage of GDP since 1955, as Figure 5 shows. Even in absolute terms, revenue has been decreasing since 2005, well before the onset of the financial crisis.[8]

Furthermore, the share of advertising in overall newspaper revenues has decreased sharply. In the United States, it has literally collapsed since the early 2000s, and it is by no means out of the question that advertising will soon account for significantly less than half of overall newspaper revenues (see Figure 6).

Indeed, this is already the case with the *New York Times,* where since 2010 advertising has accounted for less than half the paper's revenue. Since then, nearly

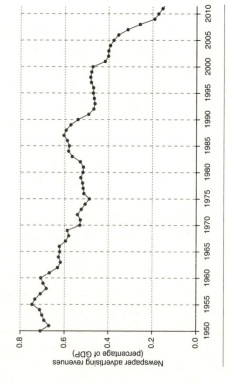

FIGURE 5. Newspaper advertising revenue as a percentage of GDP in the United States, 1950–2013

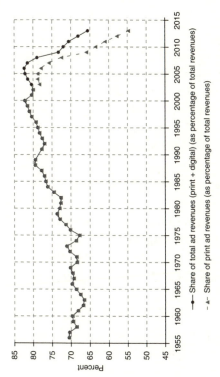

FIGURE 6. Share of advertising revenue as a percentage of total newspaper revenue in the United States, 1956–2013

— Share of total ad revenues (print + digital) (as percentage of total revenues)
-▲- Share of print ad revenues (as percentage of total revenues)

all of the increase in revenue has come from subscriptions. In France over the past forty years, advertising has never accounted for more than half of newspaper income. Since 2000, advertising's share has decreased by more than 10 percentage points (from more than 45 percent to just 35). It is also interesting to note that while advertising's share of total revenue held its own for a few years at the beginning of this century, it began to decrease rapidly in 2006, even if one includes revenue from online ads.

The media have therefore sought to innovate by proposing new forms of advertising to potential buyers. Native advertising is the downside of this innovation. At first only new media such as BuzzFeed engaged in native advertising, which accounted for nearly all the site's profit in 2013, but lately even the most prestigious papers have joined in. For example, the *New York Times,* despite having been quick to denounce the practice (which David Carr called "journalism's new peril" in 2013), published its first native ads (for Dell computers) in January 2014.[9] Since then it has published a growing number of such ads under the rubric Paid Posts. Native ads now account for 10 percent of the paper's revenue from online advertising, and that share seems likely to grow. The new media have followed suit. Thus, Vox Media recently announced Chorus for Advertisers, which will allow brand names to use its noted Chorus platform to produce native content. Politico simultaneously announced its new Politico Focus.

The problem for the media is not the size of the online advertising market—which generates $43 billion in revenue in the United States—but the fact that most of the pie goes to just a few firms. Half the local ad market is now claimed by such major web presences as Google and Facebook, soon quite likely to be joined by Amazon. Only a quarter of local ad revenue and less than 12 percent of the online ad market overall goes to newspapers.[10] This explains why Facebook's decision to publish entire news articles (with its Instant Articles service) is so important. Although this will certainly increase the readership of partner sites such as the *New York Times, National Geographic,* and BuzzFeed, the real issue is how ad revenue will be divided.

The Illusion of Competition

Newspapers lived for many years on advertising revenue, and for much of that time they made money. Some, in France and elsewhere, made a lot of money. Owning a newspaper in the nineteenth century

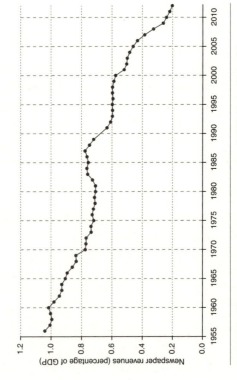

FIGURE 7. Newspaper revenue as a percentage of GDP in the United States, 1956–2013

virtually guaranteed a substantial return on investment. But times have changed, and it is a pipe dream to think that investments in media will continue to earn returns comparable to those of the past.

Not only has ad revenue collapsed in recent years, but income overall has decreased. In the United States, for example, newspaper revenue represented more than 1 percent of GDP in 1956, compared with barely 0.2 percent today, and all signs point to this decrease continuing (Figure 7). In 2013 all newspapers combined took in $32 billion, half of Google's gross revenue.

With the decline in gross revenue, newspapers also became less profitable. Why? Part of the reason is of course the decrease in advertising revenue. But most of the decline in profit is due to intensified competition in the media sector and to the structure of the industry.

The Limits of Competition

In most industries, firms respond to a decline in sales or revenue by cutting jobs. If an auto manufacturer sells fewer vehicles, the assembly line slows, and the company lays off redundant workers without affecting the quality of the cars being produced. In

other words, the number of workers needed to man-
ufacture the product varies with demand: the firm
produces fewer cars with fewer workers.

The media sector is different. No matter how many
copies a newspaper sells, the number of journalists
needed to produce it remains more or less the same.
The same subjects must be covered. Most of the effort
goes into creating the first copy, and reproduction
costs are negligible. If a paper cuts its newsroom staff
to compensate for falling revenue, quality inevitably
decreases. As we have seen, the number of journalists
employed by a media organization strongly correlates
with the quantity of news it produces (as well as the
quality). The same reasoning applies to broadcast
news (radio and television).

To put it in more technical terms, the media industry faces high fixed costs, which are a function of
the quality (or quantity) of the news produced. Hence,
media companies enjoy what economists call *increasing returns to scale:* the cost of production increases
with quality but not with the size of the market
served.[11] This provides all media companies with a
strong incentive to maximize their market share in
order to increase their revenue without increasing
production costs to the same degree. The *Guardian*
has recognized the wisdom of a strategy aimed at

increasing market size: it now operates a website in the United States that employs about sixty journalists in order to penetrate a new market far larger than its traditional British market. The *New York Times* used its dominant position in the English-speaking press to expand its market throughout the world with the *International Herald Tribune,* now rebaptized the *International New York Times.*[12]

Indeed, the monopolistic temptation—the politically correct term is *consolidation*—has frequently proved irresistible in the media sector. In the good old days, many press magnates built media empires because maximizing the size of the market meant minimizing competition. William Randolph Hearst, who acquired the *San Francisco Examiner,* the *New York (Morning) Journal,* and the *Chicago Examiner,* served as the inspiration for Orson Welles's *Citizen Kane.* Warren Buffett's holding company Berkshire Hathaway has acquired numerous newspapers in recent years: after buying the *Omaha World Herald* and associated titles in 2011, it purchased the sixty-three papers of the Media General group in 2012 and then in 2013 added the *Tulsa World,* the *News & Record,* and other titles to its portfolio. Rupert Murdoch's media empire extends from Australia (the *Herald Sun* and the *Australian*) to the United States (Fox News, the

Wall Street Journal, and the *New York Post*), and the United Kingdom (BSkyB, the *Sun,* the *Times,* and the *Sunday Times*).[13]

Eli Noam, who has studied the changing concentration of the American media, argues that business cycles and technological innovation explain how things have evolved. Faced with high fixed costs and near-zero marginal costs, the media industry must seek economies of scale and develop strategies based on economies of scope and differentiation.[14]

Yet existing legislation in France and the United States seeks to encourage competition in the media rather than consolidation. In 1986 France made it illegal for any one person or corporation to control publications with circulations exceeding 30 percent of the total national circulation. In the United States, the law is even stricter. Cross-ownership is prohibited: in any given local market, no company is allowed to own both print and broadcast media.[15]

There are many reasons for such laws. Competition in the media sector guarantees the pluralism of ideas and the freedom of information. It may even help bring out the "truth."[16] If a media company or group were to achieve a monopoly, it would be dangerous for democracy. The first risk is clearly a state monopoly over the diffusion of news. When the state-owned Office de Radiodiffusion-Télévision Française (ORTF) and the BBC enjoyed a monopoly of radio and television broadcasting in France and the United Kingdom, respectively, they were regularly accused (often justifiably) of lacking independence from the government. The television series *The Hour* vividly portrays many attempts by the British government of the 1950s to intervene in broadcasting by way of Anthony Eden's (fictional) press aide Angus McCain, much to the dismay of characters Freddie Lyon and Bel Rowley.

A private monopoly would present similar dangers. Indeed, the danger would be twofold. First, the danger of capture is greater when there is a monopoly: it is easier to corrupt one newspaper than ten newspapers, and competition gives papers an incentive to beat the competition by aiming for scoops rather than currying political favor.[17] Second, when one person controls a monopoly, that person will always be suspected of trying to influence how the news is presented. The problems raised by monopoly rents must also be considered.

Have we entered "the age of giants," and if so, does this constitute a threat to pluralism and democracy?[18] The reality is more complex. Despite the existence of media giants, competition in the media sector has in fact increased with the emergence of new actors, especially online actors such as Google and social media. They have absorbed most of the online ad revenue that once nourished traditional media. The dominance of media giants has not led to the consolidation that some observers hastily predicted. Instead, newspapers have been forced to fend for themselves.

In 2013 Rupert Murdoch split his media empire into two parts: News Corp encompassed all the Murdoch-owned newspapers and magazines while 21st Century Fox absorbed his cable, television, satellite, and film assets. In 2014 the Tribune Company separated its television assets (now Tribune Media Company) from its newspapers (Tribune Publishing) while Time Warner shed its print magazine (Time Inc.) in order to concentrate on television, film, and the Internet. The merger of E. W. Scripps and Journal Communications led to the spinoff of their newspaper properties and the creation in 2015 of two new companies: E. W. Scripps, which boasts one of the largest portfolios of television properties in the United States, and the Journal Media Group. Also in 2015, Gannett, the owner of eighty-one newspapers, including *USA Today,* announced that it would separate its press activities from its other businesses. In

France the Lagardère Group has adopted a similar strategy.

A number of newspaper companies have also chosen to refocus their core businesses. For example, the New York Times Company sold its radio and television stations and divested itself of the *Boston Globe* and other local papers in order to focus on its *New York Times* brand.

The Perverse Effects of Competition

What is the actual impact of competition in the media sector? How has increased competition in the news market affected not only the quality of the news on offer but also political participation?[19] The impact of competition depends on how it affects the incentives to produce information. Beyond a certain point, an increase in the number of competitors can lead to a decrease in both the quantity and the quality of information produced. This happens when the underlying heterogeneity of preferences for information is relatively small compared to the economies of scale so that the destructive effects of competition (staff reductions and duplication of production costs) outweigh the positive effects (improved ability to satisfy heterogeneous demand and a diversified readership).

What do I mean by "underlying heterogeneity of preferences for information"? In less technical terms, if all the consumers in a given market have exactly the same taste for information (or the same political preferences) and are prepared to pay exactly the same price for a newspaper (in which case we say they have *homogeneous* preferences), then a new paper entering the market will not bring in new readers. The existing readers will be divided between the new paper and the old, and the circulation of each paper will be smaller than the circulation of the old paper alone. In contrast, if some consumers are prepared to pay a higher price for a quality newspaper, while others prefer a less expensive paper, or if some consumers want to read a left-wing paper, while others prefer a right, then we say their preferences are *heterogeneous.* In that case, if a quality paper enters a market previously served only by a low-cost paper, new readers will emerge, both papers may achieve a satisfactory level of circulation, and the supply of news will better match the demand.

In my study of the daily regional press in France between 1945 and 2012, I showed that the entry of a new competitor led to staff cuts of up to 60 percent by the paper that previously had the market to itself, with negligible impact on the total number of journalists employed in the market (including the new entrant). The more socially homogeneous the population of the *département* in question, the stronger the effect. In other words, increased competition did not decrease the total number of journalists employed, but that total was distributed among more newspapers. A content analysis of the full text of these regional dailies also shows that the larger the number of papers in a given market, the smaller the number of articles that each one publishes, the shorter the articles, and the smaller their news content.

Furthermore, I found that the entry of a new paper and the decrease in news content due to that entry led to a decrease in participation in municipal elections. More specifically, the historical decrease in political participation over the last few decades was significantly greater in départements where newspaper competition was more intense. Although these results must be interpreted cautiously, they suggest that the intensification of competition in the media sector (broadly defined) can explain a significant part of the decline in political participation. Why? Because intensified competition led to newsroom staff reductions and thus to an inevitable decrease in the quantity of news produced by each individual news organization. Citizens were therefore less well informed, and some chose to stay away from the polls as a consequence.

What can we conclude from this analysis? A given market can support only a limited number of media organizations while sustaining the high-quality news production on which democracy depends. I do not claim to be able to predict the precise number of competitors that a given market can support. The question is complex and depends on far too many parameters (such as market size, consumer preferences, demand for ad space, mean income, and so on), so no general diagnosis is possible.

Nevertheless, the issue of *limits to competition* is sufficiently important that it cannot be ignored. An ever-growing number of media outlets do not necessarily mean better news. From this it does not follow, however, that monopoly is the solution—quite the contrary, for the reasons discussed previously. Yet it would be a mistake to argue that the crisis of the media can be resolved by multiplying the number of media actors.

The Illusion of Vast Internet Audiences

What is perhaps most surprising in the current crisis is the optimistic attitude of some newspaper editors.

Their argument is always the same: there have never been more newspaper readers. In France, for example, editors point to an explosion in the number of visitors to newspaper websites. Between 2008 and 2013, the average number of page views increased from 50 million to 180 million per site—more than tripling in five years. This is clearly a success and a reason to rejoice. Some sites, such as *Le Monde* and *Le Figaro*, have been especially successful, drawing more 600 million visitors a year. These figures are vertiginous compared to the print circulation of the same papers, which is measured in hundreds of thousands rather than millions. In July 2014 the number of monthly page views on LeMonde.fr surpassed 66 million for the first time. In January 2015, after the terror attack on the satirical weekly *Charlie Hebdo,* the number surpassed 100 million.

Was this a triumph? Yes and no. Let's take a closer look at the numbers. First, to measure the true audience of newspaper websites, it is better to look at the number of unique visitors rather than the total number of page views (a visitor can return to the site several times each day). In the case of *Le Monde,* the number of unique monthly visitors is more than 8 million, and each visitor visits the site an average of eight times per month. The average number of unique daily visitors is 1.5 million. In the United States, the *New York Times* website (NYTimes.com) had 54 million unique visitors in January 2015, which equates to fewer than 7 million daily visitors.

What can we say about the number of print readers? The circulation figures for these papers (300,000 for *Le Monde;* 650,000 for the *New York Times*) are much smaller than the web numbers. But several remarks are in order. First, circulation figures do not tell us the number of readers of the print edition. To figure that, we have to multiply the circulation by the average number of readers of each copy of the paper: six for *Le Monde* and 6.5 for the *New York Times* (according to available estimates). In other words, the average daily readership of *Le Monde* on paper is 1.8 million, while for the *Times* it is 4.2 million. In contrast to conventional wisdom, the print and web readerships are of the same order of magnitude.

Furthermore, readers devote more time to the print version of the news. The average visitor to the *Le Monde* website views only four pages and even then, only skims the online news. Web readers spend, on average, fewer than five minutes a day on the site and less than a minute on each page. The average reader spends fifty-four minutes a month on online news sites (twenty minutes on the *Le Monde* site) or a few minutes per day. The figure for the *New York Times* site is only 4.6 minutes. In contrast, readers spend twenty-five to thirty-five minutes reading printed papers.

It should now be clear why, despite the millions of claimed readers, ad revenue for online sites remains modest. In 2012 websites still accounted for less than 5 percent of total newspaper revenue in France. Newspapers have simply not been able to monetize their digital readerships, even when they charge subscription fees. A print reader generates twenty times as much ad revenue as an online reader.[20] The enormous differences in advertising charges reflect the fact that web readers spend less time reading and, more generally, that advertisers lack the historical perspective necessary to interpret what the web numbers really mean in terms of reader engagement.

Further evidence that online readers are less "valuable" can be seen in the fact that some newspapers charge less for print subscriptions than for online subscriptions (even though home delivery is far more costly for the paper than providing web access or allowing a PDF download). One such paper is the *Greensboro News and Record* (a North Carolina daily owned by Berkshire Hathaway), for which a print subscription costs 10 percent less than a digital subscription. Similarly, the *Orange County Register,* a California daily, charges more for an online-only subscription than for an online subscription combined with delivery of the Sunday print edition. In other words, readers are being subsidized to read the print version of the paper! Even the *New York Times* seems to have chosen this path: a subscription to the Sunday paper gives access to all online services at a price below that of online access alone.[21]

Of course, it is tempting to try to explain these policies by arguing that newspapers are attempting to woo their readers back to print. What they primarily signify, however, is that the real cost to the paper of an online reader is higher than the cost of a print reader because the latter comes with a subsidy in the form of ad revenue—while the former does not.

The "all news is free" model is therefore likely to prove to be a mirage. Newspapers will not escape the crisis by expanding their (nonpaying) online readership because they cannot monetize digital readers through advertising. They should instead emphasize quality as an incentive to readers to pay for content (whether through print or online subscriptions) because in the future most revenue will come from subscriptions (and newsstand sales), not from harried online browsers.

One possible objection to this argument is that no one is willing to pay for news today because it is available everywhere for free. But in fact, newspapers such as the *New York Times* have successfully established paywalls. This can be costly in terms of both time and money. It takes capital to test different models and adapt strategies to specific readerships, and owners must be prepared to take financial risks rather than seek short-term profits. Nevertheless, paid content is undoubtedly the future for an industry that has seen its advertising revenue shrink. Indeed, 41 percent of US newspapers have already established paywalls, and the paid-content model is likely to spread even more widely in coming years.

Money is the lifeblood of the media, whether it comes from print subscriptions, online subscriptions, or (in diminishing amounts) advertising. The necessary money will not come from taxing citizens "to pony up for those guys," as Bruno Ledoux, the businessman-investor who claimed to save *Libération,* once referred to the paper's journalists. Here, we encounter another of those illusions that regularly pollute the debate about the future of the media: the idea that the media are supported by the taxpayer's dollar or euro.

The Illusion of Subsidized Media

Do the media survive on government life support? Subsidies to the press are numerous and complex, especially in France. The subvention system needs to be simplified: I will offer some proposals to that end later on. But for now, it is important to be clear about the actual role subsidies play. Instead of denouncing them, we need to rethink them—and in some countries increase them.[22]

Press subsidies long predate the crisis. In France they date back to 1920, when newspapers selling for less than twenty-five centimes received a tax break. Over the years the system of subsidies evolved considerably. Until 1973 the principle was that state intervention in this sector had to be neutral: in other words, all newspapers had to be treated equally, without distinction as to content or opinion.[23] Indirect subsidies (in the form of reduced value-added taxes or postage fees) were preferred to direct subsidies.

In other countries, state intervention mostly took the form of indirect subsidies. In most European countries, newspapers benefit from a reduced value-added tax (VAT).[24] Although it is widely believed that UK newspapers are not subsidized by the government, they in fact pay zero VAT, which amounts to an effective subsidy of 838 million euros.

In the United States, the champion of free enterprise, newspapers also benefit from numerous tax breaks. They have also enjoyed reduced postage rates since the Postal Act of 1792. In Australia, New South Wales adopted legislation in 1825 that made it possible to sell newspapers at substantially lower prices— or even to give them away for free from 1835 to 1901.

In addition to such indirect subsidies, many European countries subsidize their newspapers directly in one way or another. For example, Sweden offers two types of assistance: an operating subsidy that is currently paid to eighty-seven daily papers and a distribution subsidy that goes to 134 publications. In Norway most subsidies go to the paper that is second in circulation in each local market as well as to the smallest paper in certain isolated regions. The Norwegian system also supports national papers that offer dissident and controversial political views. The goal is to maintain pluralism in the press and thus "subsidize" democracy.[25]

Finally, some governments support the newspaper industry in a more roundabout manner. In the United

Kingdom, for example, David Baines recounts how the Newspaper Society (today the News Media Association) blocked a 2006 proposal by the BBC to put news videos online because they would have competed with local papers.[26] And newspapers all over the world receive indirect support from government advertisements and legal notices.

The True Importance of Press Subsidies

Thus, the press enjoys government support almost everywhere, though with significant differences from country to country. But just how important are press subsidies?

In France, reputedly the country with the highest press subsidies, aid to the press figures in three budget lines (subsidies for distribution, modernization, and pluralism) representing a sum of 419 million euros in 2012. In addition the press benefits from another 265 million in tax expenditures, primarily in the form of a substantially reduced VAT of just 2.1 percent. Finally, the French government supports the AFP to the tune of 117.9 million euros annually. All told, press subsidies amounted to 800 million euros in 2012. Is that a lot or a little? At first sight, 800 million is a lot more than the 55 million spent by the Danish government or the 40 million spent by the Norwegian government. But to measure the importance of press subsidies in a meaningful way, we have to compare these numbers with gross revenues in the sector.

In France, 800 million euros is a little more than 9 percent of total press revenue. If we exclude support to the AFP (which benefits newspapers only indirectly), the subsidies still total 7.8 percent of gross revenue. This is partly due to the fact that press subsidies go not only to general-interest daily newspapers but also to free newspapers, magazines, the technical and professional press, and so on. All told, several thousand publications receive some form of state subsidy.

If we focus exclusively on subsidies to general-interest daily newspapers (local and national), we find that these amount to 5.3 percent of gross revenue. Since 2013 the Ministry of Culture and Communication has published data on the 200 publications receiving the highest subsidies, so we can look at individual newspapers, and when we do, we find significant variations. In terms of gross revenues, subsidies vary from 1 percent for *Corse-Matin* to 23 percent for *L'Humanité*. For *Le Monde* it is more than 10 percent, and for *Libération* it is almost 17.

How do things stand elsewhere in the world? In the United States, total press subsidies (in the form of reduced postage fees and tax breaks) represent less than 3 percent of the gross revenue of daily newspapers alone and barely 1.5 percent of gross press revenue more generally (newspapers and magazines). In the Nordic countries, reputed to give more generous press subsidies, government aid represents less than 3 percent of newspaper revenue; in Norway it is 2.2 percent, and in Sweden it is 2.9.

For obvious reasons, it is difficult to be precise when making international comparisons. France seems to be at the top of the range in granting government subsidies, but subsidies everywhere are roughly comparable in size. More specifically, subsidies account for a very small fraction of gross newspaper revenues (no greater than 10 percent anywhere and generally, less than 5 percent).

Subsidies in Context

To better understand what these ratios mean, we must look at the media in the broader context of the cultural industries and the knowledge economy more generally. In particular, it is interesting to ask what share of cultural industry revenue comes from private spending and what share comes from public financing. In France in 2012, government spending on culture and communication amounted to 13.9 billion euros, or 7.2 percent of cultural production.[27]

Relative to production, state support of the press is roughly similar to the government share of spending in the culture and communication sectors overall. It is sharply lower, however, than government spending on institutions providing access to culture and knowledge (such as libraries, archives, and cultural education) and in the audiovisual sector, where it represents approximately 30 percent of production. But it is still much higher than government spending in the visual arts sector (art market, design, and photography), book publishing, architecture, and industries dealing with images and sound (recorded music, video, video games, musical instruments, and scores), where it is 1 percent. The sectors most comparable to the press in terms of public intervention include film, historical monuments, and live theater. In France, the Centre National du Cinéma et de l'Image Animée (CNC) paid out more than 300 million euros in support of the French film industry in 2015.[28] This is lower than UK support for the film industry, where "film tax relief" alone resulted in more than 300 million euros in tax breaks in 2013–2014, to which one must add financing from the British Film Institute (BFI).[29]

Furthermore, even in countries where press subsidies are relatively low, the state intervenes in the media through subsidies to the audiovisual sector. This is the case in the United Kingdom, for example, where press subsidies (in the form of reduced VAT) amounted to less than thirteen euros per capita in 2014–2015, but public financing of audiovisual media exceeded eighty euros per capita (primarily from the license fee).[30] It remains to be seen whether this strong public support of the BBC will be challenged by British Conservatives after their victory in the May 2015 legislative elections. Prime Minister David Cameron's choice for culture secretary, John Whittingdale, has been a vigorous critic of the use of the license fee to finance the BBC. He has said that the license fee is "worse than the poll tax" instituted under Margaret Thatcher. All signs are that deep cuts are in the offing.

Only in the United States is government intervention small in both the print media and the audiovisual sector. Total public financing of the Corporation for Public Broadcasting (CPB), which supports public radio and television in the United States, amounted to less than three euros per capita in 2012, with the federal government's share less than 1.2 euros per

American.[31] Furthermore, indirect US public support for the press (through reduced postal fees and tax breaks) is less than three euros per person.

FINALLY, IT IS interesting to compare what newspapers receive from the state with what they give back to the state. Indeed, newspapers, like other firms, pay a great deal to the state in the form of taxes, fees, and social insurance contributions. Consider the French case, for which abundant data are available. I will concentrate once again on the 200 national and regional dailies that receive the most state aid. On average, the aid provided to these publications amounts to less than 60 percent of what they pay to the state in taxes, and even this figure is inflated by certain publications that receive particularly large subsidies: the median is only 35 percent. In other words, newspapers (with few exceptions) pay the state much more than they receive. If we look at national dailies such as *Les Échos, La Croix, Le Figaro,* and *Aujourd'hui en France,* the ratio of subsidies to taxes varies from 42 to 62 percent. In 2012, however, it was 113 percent for *Le Monde,* 117 percent for *L'Humanité,* and 146 percent for *Libération.*

The main conclusion of this analysis is the following: when placed in the perspective of the economy as a whole, the press is not a subsidized sector but a sector that is taxed at an overall lower rate than other sectors in France and other developed countries.

Indeed, other participants in the knowledge economy, such as universities and research centers, receive more public than private financing (from tuition fees and research contracts, for example) and, a fortiori, much more than they pay in taxes. In some countries they also receive income from their capital endowments, which they have amassed in part through public assistance (especially in the form of favorable tax treatment). This model could also apply to the media if the law were changed to allow them to take advantage of it. In short the question is not whether the media should be subsidized. It is rather whether they should be granted a favorable legal and tax status in recognition of their contribution to democracy—a status comparable to that long enjoyed by many other participants in the knowledge economy.

Reforming Subsidies to the Press

In France the problem lies not with the size of press subsidies as such but rather with the form they take and the absence of targeting. As noted previously, Sweden subsidizes the operating costs of eighty-seven daily papers and the distribution costs of 134. Under the legal framework that governs the press in France, nearly all print publications benefit from large VAT reductions and reduced postage fees—some 9,000 titles in all, fewer than 400 of which are general-interest newspapers.

Because of the size of the postal subsidy, we find among the 200 publications receiving the largest subsidies in 2012 ten television magazines, five of which number among the twenty-five most highly subsidized titles. And this does not even count the VAT reduction, 61 percent of which goes to publications that are not general-interest newspapers.[32] If we look at all forms of subsidies to the press (including tax expenditures), we find that 35 percent goes to mass-circulation print magazines.

Reform of press subsidies in France should therefore begin by replacing the present system, which is overly complex and burdened by contradictory objectives, with a simpler, more automatic system under which subsidies would be based on a newspaper's gross revenue or circulation. Subsidies would go only to general-interest newspapers, considerably reducing the cost to the state. In Chapter 3, I will propose a more extensive reform that could be applied in countries other than France.

In the United States, the government needs to devote more resources to the media. As noted, American subsidies to both the press and the audiovisual media are low and have actually fallen sharply over the past few decades. For example, the postal subsidy was cut by more than 80 percent under the Postal Reorganization Act of 1970. In the current crisis, many academics and journalists such as Robert McChesney, John Nichols, and Lee Bollinger have called for higher government subsidies but continue to argue about the optimal form of such aid.[33, 34] One idea is that the media should, in the future, be considered a part of the nonprofit sector. Meanwhile, various wealthy investors have poured millions into the media. Some have proposed that such investors be treated like donors to nonprofits and granted tax breaks. Is this a good idea? In order to answer this question, we must first examine yet another illusion: the idea that a new golden age has arrived for the media.

The Illusion of a New Golden Age

Jeff Bezos, Pierre Omidyar, John Henry—do these names mean anything to you? If not, you should know that many people regard these billionaires as the future of the American media. With their deep pockets, they have invested millions in media ventures in recent years, reviving undercapitalized companies and infusing new life into newsrooms.

Pierre Omidyar, the founder of eBay, invested nearly $250 million in First Look Media, a hybrid venture combining a nonprofit news operation with a for-profit high-tech enterprise. With a staff of twenty-some experienced journalists, including Glenn Greenwald, best known for publishing Edward Snowden's revelations about the National Security Agency, he launched the *Intercept,* a magazine of online investigative journalism.

John Henry, an American investor and the owner of the Boston Red Sox, purchased the *Boston Globe* for $70 million while Doug Manchester, a real-estate promoter, bought the *San Diego Union-Tribune* (subsequently renamed *U-T San Diego*) for $100 million. Similar acquisitions have occurred in France. Xavier Niel, the primary stockholder in Free (a telephone and Internet company) and one of the wealthiest people in France, is part owner of *Le Monde* and *Le Nouvel Observateur* and an investor in Mediapart. Another billionaire telecom investor, Patrick Drahi, rescued *Libération*, then acquired the Roularta Media

Group, which publishes *L'Express,* and eventually became the controlling shareholder of NextRadioTV who owns a number of French radio and television channels (including news channel BFMTV and radio channel RMC), thus creating a veritable media empire that includes both print and broadcast media.

Finally, Jeff Bezos, the founder and CEO of Amazon, bought the *Washington Post,* a pillar of American journalism, in October 2013 for $250 million—a pittance for a man whose personal fortune is estimated at nearly $30 billion. Is this good news? The purchase of the *Post* has guaranteed that the paper's journalists will have the resources and independence they need for many years to come. Despite many newsroom layoffs in previous years, the paper can now invest and hire new staff for its revamped website, open a nighttime news desk, and field a team to report on breaking news. The new owner's cash infusion will allow the *Post* to become an experimental laboratory for the digital age, to reflect on its operations, and to search for a new model for the newspapers of the future.

The Death of One Kind of Freedom

All this new investment in the media has drawn enthusiastic applause. Some see the interest of these billionaire investors as the harbinger of a new golden age: once again, newspapers will be flush with resources and staff. Unfortunately, there is no guarantee that these generous new investors are not out to acquire tools to enhance their own influence. Worse, they may be seeking merely to amuse themselves. Our nostalgia for the great family dynasties that used to dominate the media may have led us to forget that what they really represented was the concentration of power. While Harrison Gray Otis and Harry Chandler were quite conscious of their public-service mission as owners of the *Los Angeles Times,* they also—some would say above all—used the newspaper to further their own political and economic interests. The film *Chinatown* tells us more than many a lengthy tome about how Harry Chandler built his financial empire. And then of course there is *Citizen Kane.*

There have always been wealthy people prepared to dabble in the media, but their newfound prominence poses a genuine problem for democracy. There is no denying that these wealthy investors have infused new life and energy into the media. But if the media of the future must depend on wealthy investors for their financing, many dangers lie ahead.

Why? Let us approach the problem in a roundabout way by considering the way political campaigns are financed. In most democracies, campaign financing is governed by strict rules. In particular, the size of individual gifts to political parties is limited. This is the case in Canada, for example. In France physical persons cannot give more than 7,500 euros to any political party or group, and total household contributions may not exceed 15,000 euros per year. Contributions to an individual candidate or candidates may not exceed 4,600 euros per election. In the United States, until 2014, individual contributions to federal campaigns were limited to $123,000 per election cycle of two years. Within that overall limit, individual contributions could not exceed $2,600 per candidate, and total gifts to candidates could not exceed $48,600. Furthermore, contributions to political action committees (PACs) were limited to $5,000 per candidate per election cycle.[35]

Why impose such limits? In order to prevent financial pressure on parties and candidates that might compromise their independence. Worries about such corruption are so pervasive that they have made their way into fiction. In the Danish television series *Borgen,* Birgitte Nyborg creates her own New Democrat Party, but when she seeks financing she discovers that one very generous offer comes with unacceptable strings attached (the donor wants her to change important parts of her economic program). This episode illustrates the way money can compromise the basic principle of democratic debate (one person, one vote).

If you prefer history to fiction, any number of examples from the American past show how a privileged minority can use its money for political advantage. A 2010 decision of the Supreme Court removed all ceilings on donations to so-called Super PACs, political action committees supposedly without attachment to any party or candidate. In the 2012 presidential election, this decision allowed some $1.3 billion in outside financing to influence the political process. Super PACs can raise and spend unlimited funds to support a candidate because the requirement that they maintain nominal independence is flouted in practice. And they operate in the shadows because contributors can remain anonymous. This encourages corporate contributions and corrupts the entire political system.[36]

One person, one vote? Scholars have recently shown that one reason the American political system has failed to prevent the rise of inequality in recent decades is that wealthy contributors have used their money to influence the electoral and legislative process. The wealthiest 0.01 percent of households capture almost 5 percent of total national income, but these same households are responsible for more than 40 percent of political contributions.[37] What are the consequences? Martin Gilens has shown that when the preferences of the poorest 10 percent and of the middle class diverge from the preferences of the wealthy, government policy responds only to the preferences of the wealthy.[38]

Similarly, the millions that wealthy individuals (and corporations) have invested in the media undermine the workings of democracy, which depends in important ways on providing voters with high-quality and unbiased information. Surely, it is no accident that the same people are often both large political contributors and major media investors. The most striking examples are the Koch brothers. Charles and David Koch are American billionaires who made their money in petrochemicals. (More precisely, they inherited an oil company founded by their father, and each of the brothers is today worth an estimated $36 billion.) The two brothers are major financiers of the Tea Party and also maintain close ties to Fox News, whose majority stockholder, Rupert Murdoch, has contributed generously to Republican political campaigns for decades.

Even if the motives of these wealthy investors are pure—saving the media, supplying a quality public good, and earning a return on their capital in an industry in which they truly believe—what about their children? No one can be sure what the next generation will want: the fact that heirs are capricious is the main problem with the idea that we are witnessing a new golden age for the media. Relying on generous investors is no way to finance the media on a durable basis. Indeed, when the time came to pass ownership to a new generation, the major American newspapers were forced to sell their shares on the stock exchange, which proved to be an unfortunate error.

In France it was in part Claude Perdriel's worries about what his heirs would do with "his" *Nouvel Observateur* that caused him to finally decide to sell his shares. And it was in part the settlement of the estate of the Italian publisher Carlo Caracciolo that plunged the newspaper *Libération* into the crisis in which it finds itself today. That is why it is preferable for media companies to be organized as foundations rather than joint-stock companies: in a foundation, heirs cannot dispose freely of capital they inherit. The investment is *irrevocable,* hence permanent.

To sum up, let me note that French political parties today are financed primarily by state subsidies, and in the United States many people favor a reform of the campaign finance laws to make public financing the exclusive means of funding political campaigns. The idea that politics should not be governed by the laws of the market is taking hold. Candidates, voters, and government policies are not commodities or investments. Similarly, the information on which citizens rely for enlightened democratic debate cannot be left at the mercy of the market.

· 3 ·

A NEW MODEL FOR THE
TWENTY-FIRST CENTURY

Can't we imagine a press owned in a disinterested
way by a vast society of readers to which each
member would contribute regularly, or else by a
foundation of the sort that is so common in the
United States? In the latter case, the generous
donors would of course forfeit the right and ability
to intervene in the management of the newspaper. They would thus demonstrate, to their advantage, the purity of their intentions and place
themselves beyond suspicion.

—Hubert Beuve-Méry Ambassadors' Lecture, 1956

ONE CAN ALWAYS DREAM. Indeed, with many news
outlets now mired in crisis, it has become imperative
to think of new models for the media. The one I will
propose here is based on crowdfunding and power-
sharing. I hope that it may serve as a new economic
and legal template for the media of the twenty-first
century, a template that combines aspects of both a

joint-stock company and a foundation. Let us call this new entity a *nonprofit media organization* (NMO).

The debate about the legal status of media organizations is not new, but in the age of the Internet and crowdfunding, new thinking is required. To begin, it is useful to recall some mistakes of the past, starting with the experience of newspapers that have become publicly held corporations.

Transcending the Laws of the Market

Media companies are not like other companies. Their primary purpose is not to maximize profits and pay dividends to stockholders but to provide a public good: the free, unbiased, high-quality information that is indispensable to democratic debate. Or perhaps I should say, rather, that media companies *ought* not to be like other companies, because when they are it is usually to the detriment of the information they provide.

Honoré de Balzac's story *La peau de chagrin* revolves around a magical piece of hide (the *peau* of the title) on which are inscribed the words, "If you possess me, you possess everything." Every wish will be granted to the person who owns this piece of skin. But the price is high: "Your life will belong to me." The story of the American press and the stock exchange provides a good illustration of this kind of magic. After 1960 shares of a number of American newspapers began to trade on the stock exchange: Dow Jones & Company (which then owned the *Wall Street Journal*) in 1963, the New York Times Company (which then published the *Boston Globe* as well as the *New York Times*), the Gannett Company (*USA Today*) in 1967, the Washington Post Company in 1971, and so on.

The idea of taking these companies public initially seemed reasonable. For the heirs of the founders of these media dynasties, who faced substantial estate taxes and were perhaps less interested in public service than their forebears, going public meant reaping a financial windfall. What is more, some families were able to enjoy this windfall without forfeiting power over their newspapers by issuing two classes of shares: one that was publicly traded and another that conferred greater voting rights (usually in a ratio of ten to one), with the latter reserved for the founders and their descendants.

In addition, going public was a quick and efficient way to raise capital at a time when newspapers needed cash to purchase new technologies (to transition from linotype to photocomposition, for example). It was also a quick and efficient way to build a media empire using shares rather than cash for mergers and acquisitions, as Gannett did.[1]

But there was a price to pay. Going public proved to be a mistake both for the newspapers themselves and for democracy. Paradoxically, however, newspaper profits initially increased. When the consequences of going public were first assessed in the 1990s, operating margins were found to have risen from 10 to 15 percent of gross revenue to 20 to 30 percent or more.[2] Unfortunately, this turned out to be not good news (except of course for investors, who initially saw stock prices and dividends rise sharply).

In reality, the improved margins came as a result of harsh austerity measures: costs were cut and newsroom staffs slashed, which, unsurprisingly, affected the quality of the news. That this was indeed the case is obvious from the fact that cash flow and profits increased more rapidly than gross revenues: profits were raised by cutting costs at the expense of quality. In the first five years after the *Chicago Tribune* went public, profits rose at the rate of 23 percent per year while gross revenue increased at a rate of only 9 percent; this performance was achieved by slashing expenditures drastically.[3] Thus, the magical *peau de chagrin* inexorably shrank.

Improved profits also came at the expense of democracy. After newspapers went public, their circulation decreased. What may be surprising is that investors were glad about this. Why? Because in many cases, the decrease was the result of a deliberate strategy: newspapers aimed their content at wealthier readers in order to increase their advertising revenue. Recall that until the early 2000s, advertising accounted for 80 percent of the revenue of American newspapers. This led to market segmentation and to increased prices for newspapers. Above all, it left a growing number of people without a source of news.

These people were deprived in two ways. As newspaper prices increased, poorer readers could no longer afford them. Furthermore, certain communities were abandoned by the media (or, more precisely, by advertisers), creating a veritable news void. The drive for higher profits affected not just newspapers but local radio and television outlets as well (some television stations have operating margins above 50 percent), and the imperative to produce quality local news fell by the wayside.[4] This took place, moreover, despite the fact that broadcasters are ostensibly required to devote part of their airtime to local public affairs. But this requirement has never been seriously enforced in the United States.[5]

When advertising revenue collapsed in the early 2000s, especially in the general-interest press, the utter bankruptcy of this strategy was revealed. Newspapers discovered that they could not rely on income from advertising, and publicly traded companies saw their profitability plummet. They paid a heavy price for their profit-maximization strategy. The resulting decrease in quality turned off potential readers, who were no longer willing to pay for the kind of news that was being produced. Newspapers thus lost out with both investors and readers. Some media empires then dumped their newspaper assets. Media companies suffered and so did democracy.

The Market

The news media must somehow transcend the laws of the market. The race for higher profits led media companies to neglect their primary purpose, which is to supply unbiased, high-quality information. To put it bluntly: shares of news media companies should not be publicly traded. This is particularly true in the United States, where publicly held companies have a fiduciary responsibility to their stockholders to maximize profits. This legal obligation conflicts with their moral responsibility to "serve the general welfare" (as indicated in the Statement of Principles of the American Society of Newspaper Editors). Similarly, because universities have a moral responsibility to educate and engage in research, it is hard to imagine them as publicly traded profit-maximizing corporations.

In France serious consideration was given to taking *Le Monde* public, but in the end it did not happen. Although no French papers are publicly traded, they are nevertheless subject to the logic of the market. The vast majority of newspapers are joint-stock companies, and even in the absence of a fiduciary obligation to stockholders, many are quite obviously managed in a way that privileges profits over quality news. The people who own shares in newspapers are hardly disinterested spectators.

At the end of World War II, many people in France embraced the notion that newspapers should enjoy a special legal status. Since then, however, the idea has been honored mainly in the breach, except for occasional experiments with societies of readers, societies of journalists, and cooperative arrangements.

Nonprofit Media Organizations

In the United States, the United Kingdom, Ireland, and Germany, newspaper companies have experimented with a variety of innovative formulas over many years. Many nonprofit media organizations have emerged.

In the United States, one finds state-owned media such as the Voice of America, university-owned media (such as the *State Press* of Arizona State University, *Oklahoma Watch,* and the International Reporting Project), and media foundations, about which I will say more in a moment.

In Germany the largest media conglomerate, Bertelsmann—number one in Europe and one of the largest media companies in the world—is owned by the Bertelsmann Foundation. In case the name Bertelsmann means nothing to you, here are some figures: gross revenue of 16.4 billion euros in 2013; profit of 870 million euros; 110,000 employees. Bertelsmann occupies a significant place in the media landscape in France, in Europe and in the United States, where it is the majority shareholder in Penguin Random House, the largest publishing house in the world.[6] From 2004 to 2008, it owned half of Sony BMG, at that time the world's largest record company.

Is the Bertelsmann formula the miraculous solution to the crisis of the media? Does it offer a model for the future? It is an interesting case because it exemplifies in extreme form both the advantages and the limits of foundation status for media companies. The principal advantage is stability: foundations are based on irrevocable gifts by their founders. This is a significant plus. The Bertelsmann Foundation, created in 1977, is today the principal stockholder in the Bertelsmann media company, which dates from 1835. Reinhard Mohn, who owned the company when the foundation was created, transferred the majority of his shares to the foundation in 1993.

This gift established the company, which had always refused to go public, on a stable foundation (protecting it in particular from the problem of inheritance). Employees also benefited from this arrangement thanks to a generous profit-sharing plan. Whatever subsequent generations of heirs may wish, they cannot liquidate the shares bequeathed to the foundation. This structure has in no way impeded Bertelsmann's growth. Its creditworthiness has been evaluated by bond-rating agencies, its bonds are traded, and it also issues "profit-sharing certificates" (which can be traded as well). What are the limits of this model? To borrow from the words of Hubert Beuve-Méry quoted in the epigraph to this chapter, the "generous donors" have not forfeited either the "right" or "the ability to intervene in the management" of the media company. The profit-sharing certificates issued by the company confer no voting rights on their owners. All voting rights remain with Bertelsmann Management, which is controlled by the foundation and also exercises the family's voting rights. The president of Bertelsmann Management is Liz Mohn, the wife of Reinhard Mohn, who also serves as vice president of the foundation and its board of overseers, on which her son Christoph Mohn and daughter Brigitte Mohn also sit.

After its founding by Carl Bertelsmann in 1835, the media company was headed by Carl's son Heinrich, Heinrich's stepson Johannes Mohn, and then by four more generations of Mohns down to Reinhard, who became chairman in 1947 and died in 2009, leaving his place to his wife, Liz. Despite undeniable successes, the foundation structure was regularly used to ensure that power would remain in the family.

In this way the Bertelsmann-Mohns have maintained their power over the German media conglomerate for six generations. Is there any real difference between this strategy and that of Rupert Murdoch, who announced that he was giving up operational control of 21st Century Fox and, in the same breath, that he was passing the reins to his son James Murdoch and the vice-chairmanship to his other son Lachlan Murdoch? Why abet family control of companies through tax-advantaged family foundations?

Governance and Stock

The problem is this: foundation status does not determine how media companies are governed. The relationship between financial resources and decision-making power remains unresolved. Should power be strictly proportional to shares of capital? If so, what potential countervailing powers can exist?

In a typical joint-stock company, there is no countervailing power. Whoever owns the most shares also has the lion's share of the voting rights. This is a problem, because a dominant shareholder can see to it that the company serves his or her own economic or political agenda rather than the public interest. As noted earlier, we have a similar problem with campaign contributions, and to deal with it we have instituted fairly strict limits on the amounts that can be "invested" in political campaigns. It is difficult to impose similar limits on investments in the media, and even if it were possible to do so, it would not be desirable since the media are currently short of capital. We need to find a way to encourage invest-ment in media companies, not discourage it.

So, even though I recognize the advantages of the foundation form and in some respects draw my in-spiration from it, I want to propose a new model, that I call the *nonprofit media organization model,* which combines features of both foundations and joint-stock companies.

The purpose of this new model is twofold. The first is to bring new capital to the media (by granting at-tractive tax advantages) and to stabilize the capital base by making investments irrevocable.[7] The second is to limit the decision-making power of outside in-vestors (in exchange for which investors receive cer-tain tax breaks). This can be done by devising strict bylaws defining the place of societies of readers and employees in the governance structure and by establishing a fiscal framework to encourage crowd-funding. Under these bylaws, voting rights would cease to be proportional to shares owned (beyond a certain level of participation). In contrast, small shareholders would have their voting rights increased. The goal would be to allow for genuine turnover of power and personnel.

Before going into greater detail, let me rapidly survey existing models of nonprofit media organizations to gain a better idea of their advantages and limitations.

Existing Nonprofit Media Organizations

One of the oldest independent foundation-owned newspapers is the *Guardian,* a pillar of the British press. The *Guardian* is owned by the Guardian Media Group, which is itself entirely controlled by the Scott Trust, a nonprofit foundation whose mission since 1936 has been to safeguard the paper's independence. Similarly, the *Irish Times,* founded in 1859, has been owned by the Irish Times Trust since 1974.

In Germany, as noted previously, there is the Bertelsmann Foundation. One of the leading German dailies, the conservative *Frankfurter Allgemeine Zeitung (FAZ),* with a circulation of more than 300,000, is 93 percent owned by the FAZIT-Stiftung.

In France, *Ouest-France,* the leading daily in terms of circulation, has been owned by a nonprofit organization (called a *law of 1901 association*) since the early 1990s. With this legal status, the newspaper was able to avoid a hostile takeover (previously, shareholders had been permitted to sell their shares to the highest bidder).[8] Similarly, it was to lock down the capital of *La Montagne* and to preserve the paper's independence that led Marguerite Varenne, the widow of founder Alexander Varenne and owner of nearly 80 percent of the company's shares in 1980, to create a foundation to which she donated the majority of her stock.

However, it is in the United States, where philanthropy reigns supreme, that we find the largest number of nonprofit media organizations.[9] One of the best-known is ProPublica, a pure Internet player specializing in investigative journalism, which Herbert and Marion Sandler created in 2008 with a donation of several million dollars. The site, which began with twenty-eight journalists and now employs forty-three, has already won two Pulitzer Prizes.

This is just one example—not very representative in terms of size or success—of nonprofit journalism. Among the more successful ventures we find the *Tampa Bay Times* (formerly the *St. Petersburg Times*), which is owned by the Poynter Institute, a nonprofit school of journalism; the *Texas Tribune,* launched in 2009 and financed by a number of foundations as well as individual donations; the *Christian Science Monitor;* and of course the Associated Press, one of the world's leading press agencies and oldest cooperatives.

Can we say that the nonprofit form is *the* solution to the current crisis of the media? Notwithstanding the exceptional cases cited above, most nonprofit media companies are very small. Operating with limited staff and modest budgets, they cannot aspire to exhaustive coverage of the news. According to the Pew Research Center, the vast majority of these companies have fewer than five full-time employees; some have none. By this measure organizations like ProPublica and the Center for Investigative Reporting (with seventy-three employees) count as giants. Most of these organizations engage in *niche journalism,* specializing in narrowly defined subject areas.

Although such publications do bring welcome fresh air to democratic debate and to some extent fill the void left by cost cutting in the traditional media, they do not appear to be capable of substituting for existing newspapers, especially since most of them are pure Internet players, which suffer from the same weaknesses as newspaper websites. The average visit to the website of a nonprofit publication lasts fewer than two minutes, half the length of the average visit to the site of a traditional American paper and far less than the time spent reading a traditional print paper.[10]

These weaknesses are not intrinsically related to the foundation status of the organizations in question but are due in large part to their inadequate capitalization. Foundations deserve credit for putting readers back in the center of the picture because they do not rely on advertising revenue and are not slaves to the market, yet they have failed to involve readers in their financing. What I mean by this is simply that few media organizations, whether for-profit or nonprofit, have tried to avail themselves of large-scale crowdfunding. Except for the *Voice of San Diego,* which launched one of the largest-ever media crowdfunding campaigns (the Bigger Voice Fund), media companies have raised very little money via this route. Foundations generally favor large donations from wealthy individuals, firms, or other foundations over small individual contributions. This gives rise to two problems. First, they become vulnerable to excessive influence by a small number of individuals, thus creating a risk to democracy. And second, they become equally vulnerable to economic downturns and therefore financially fragile.

One other point deserves emphasis: the tax laws pertaining to foundations are extremely complex in both the United States and France, and this places strict limits on the development of foundation-based or other alternative media. In the United States, it is very difficult for a nonprofit news operation to meet the criteria of Section 501(c)3 of the tax code, which must be satisfied by any organization seeking to accept tax-exempt contributions and avoid payment of the corporate income tax. In particular, it is not always easy for media firms to demonstrate that they satisfy the "educational purposes" requirement.

In the United States, the media are not prima facie regarded as operating in the public interest, so if they wish to be treated as foundations they have to adopt a roundabout strategy such as forging an alliance with a foundation whose purpose is strictly educational. Hence, nearly two-thirds of nonprofit media firms in the United States are currently subsidized by other organizations (such as universities) that do meet the requirements of Section 501(c)3. Only one-third are independent. Bills (such as one filed by Sen. Ben Cardin) have been designed to make it much easier for newspapers to qualify under Section 501(c)3, but thus far these have gone nowhere.[11]

Similarly, in France the statutes governing nonprofit organizations are extremely complex. A 2008 "economic modernization law" created a new entity, the endowment fund *(fonds de dotation),* which is much simpler to set up than a foundation yet still offers a tax break to donors, but this status is not open to media organizations. Like 501(c)3 groups in the United States, endowment funds in France must operate in the public interest for a social, cultural, educational, athletic, or charitable purpose. Thus, the media are excluded. French authorities are currently considering extending foundation status to media organizations, however, and it is to be hoped that this comes to pass. One possibility would be to declare the maintenance of press pluralism as a mission in the public interest. In any case it is extremely important that we begin to think of the media as part of a much larger ecosystem, the knowledge-producing sector of the economy.

The Price of Independence

One thing we learn from the US and French examples is that we procrastinate constantly. The idea that the news media, like universities, provide a public good is increasingly widely accepted. Hence, it should be legitimate for the state to assist them and to encourage private donations via tax reductions and exemptions. Yet media companies are also private enterprises (most are joint-stock companies), hence there is no legal basis for granting them tax exemptions. And some are owned by large corporations, such as Dassault Aviation, which owns *Le Figaro,* so why shouldn't they be taxed like any other corporation?

Bear in mind, however, that the press in general, not just the news media, already enjoy certain tax advantages (such as the substantial VAT break they receive in France and other countries). Furthermore, nonprofit businesses are defined not by the absence of commercial activity but by disinterested management. In particular, any positive earnings must be reinvested in the firm and not distributed. Press earnings being what they are at the moment, this should not present any drawback.

Let us broaden our view to the knowledge economy in general. In France private organizations "whose management is disinterested and which are engaged in presenting live or cinematic performances to the public" can accept tax-deductible donations *even if they are required to pay commercial taxes*. Similarly, media companies are also private organizations that should, provided their management is similarly disinterested, be allowed to accept tax-deductible donations to support the provision of high-quality information to the general public. If the organization also engages in significant commercial activities, as is the case with the press, those activities can be split off into a commercial subsidiary.

This is not the place to delve into the legal niceties. The many technical details that would need to be covered are far beyond the scope of this book and vary widely from country to country. My point is not to propose specific improvements in French or American law. It is rather to argue that extending the tax breaks accorded to endowment funds in France and 501(c)3 organizations in the United States would mark a significant step forward. The current system for contributions to the media is too complicated. Simplification would encourage private donations and make state aid more efficient. Even more important, reorganizing media companies as foundations would make it possible to establish permanent capital endowments. Gifts to foundations are *irrevocable,* and a system of irrevocable investments would make it possible to guarantee the independence of media companies over the long run.

Limits

Despite the many merits of foundations, they do not provide answers to all the challenges facing the media. Hence, we must also reflect on new models.

Endowment funds in France can be set up with minimal legal formalities, but there is one drawback to this simplicity: there is no regulation of fund by-laws. The individuals who set up the fund can draft its bylaws in such a way as to retain all decision-making power for themselves and transmit it to their heirs (through boards of directors recruited by co-optation) without the payment of estate taxes and without interference from fund employees or outside shareholders (such as crowdfunders). If media funds are to receive tax breaks, the founders must in turn cede some of their decision-making power and agree to democratic governance.

The position of the founders is equivalent to that of majority shareholders in a corporation, hence they must agree to share power with small donors, who must be allowed to contribute to the fund's endowment, not in order to receive dividends (because there is no distribution of earnings in a nonprofit organization) but precisely in order to participate in making decisions. Power must also be shared with employees. If journalists (and other employees) contribute to the fund, then obviously they deserve a place in the organization's strategic organs, where crucial decisions are undertaken.

The type of nonprofit media organization I am proposing thus combines the virtues of different legal types. It enjoys the advantages of a foundation (stability of financing and ability to focus on information as a public good rather than on profit maximization at the expense of quality) and those of a joint-stock company (diversified ownership, replenishment of leadership ranks, and democratic decision making provided that the power of the largest shareholders is appropriately limited). Before turning to the details of my proposal, I want to review the results of various experiments with democratic governance of media organizations around the world.

Cooperatives

A number of countries have experimented with various alternatives to the straightforward joint-stock company in the media sector. In France, workers' cooperative production societies *(sociétés coopératives ouvrières de production,* or *SCOPs)* are companies in which workers join together to exercise their professions under either their own direct management or the management of elected representatives. Under the principle of one person, one vote, the *SCOPs* represent a form of workplace democracy. The regional daily *L'Yonne républicaine* was a *SCOP* from 1955 to 2008, when it was bought by Centre France; *Le Courrier picard,* another French regional daily, was a *SCOP* until 2009. In the United Kingdom, the cooperative *East End News,* a widely praised initiative of the early

1980s, lasted only a few years. The *News on Sunday* died after a few months.

In the United States, some cooperatives, such as the *Inter-County Leader* in Wisconsin (published by the Inter-County Cooperative Publishing Association) still survive. Historically, however, cooperatives in the US media sector have been rare, and the few papers that experimented with the cooperative form were small local papers with very tenuous financing.[12] Very few papers are still owned (or even partially owned) by their employees. One such is the *Gazette* of Cedar Rapids, Iowa. Until its purchase by Berkshire Hathaway in 2011, the *Omaha World-Herald* was the largest employee-owned newspaper in the United States. The employee stock ownership plan (ESOP) has never caught on in the media sector.[13]

France also has the worker shareholder corporation *(société anonyme à participation ouvrière,* or *SAPO),* where part of a firm's capital is owned by its employees.[14] This is a little-known type of organization, and apart from *La Nouvelle République du Centre-Ouest,* a *SAPO* until 2009, it has never been tried in the media sector. Although Germany has no legal entity comparable to the *SAPO,* the employees of the leading newsweekly, *Der Spiegel,* own a 50.5 percent majority interest in the firm. But there is a significant caveat:

only the journalists employed by the magazine's print edition are shareholders; employees of the website are excluded. In addition, workers in all German companies enjoy significant representation on the board of directors under the well-known *Mitbestimmung* (comanagement) arrangement.

Why have most attempts at democratic management failed, with few exceptions?[15] Take the cases of *L'Yonne républicaine* and *Le Courrier picard* in France. The financial situation of both papers deteriorated to the point where they could no longer remain independent, thus illustrating the limits of worker management. The newspaper business requires large amounts of capital and substantial investment in new technologies (offset presses, computers for the newsroom, etc.). Cooperatives may be attractive in terms of democratic governance, but this can lead to inefficient redistribution so that the coffers are empty when the time comes to invest.[16] Indeed, the only remaining French cooperative, the magazine *Alternatives économiques,* which has been a *SCOP* since 1984, stipulates in its bylaws that a substantial share of its profits must be reinvested in the firm, which has, consequently, amassed significant reserves of capital. What is more, the task of managing a firm becomes more complex as it grows in size so that the kind of democratic governance that one finds in cooperatives becomes difficult, if not impossible, in practice.

In addition, employee shareholders tend to discourage new investment. In a *SAPO,* for example, the law allows each firm to determine the respective number of shares allotted to employees and investors. Any change in the share ratio requires amendment of the firm's bylaws, for which agreement is very difficult to obtain. And cooperative status affords no guarantee of editorial independence if, for example, a controlling share is acquired by a large corporation.

The crux of the matter, then, is to strike a proper balance between a strict financial logic (one share, one vote, with no further limitation and no protection against plutocratic control) and a strict democratic logic (one vote for each employee as in a cooperative, no matter what the capital invested or personal commitment to the firm). The strict financial logic leads to the problems we have already discussed while history, unfortunately, teaches us that the cooperative logic does not work in the media sector.

Hence, it is important to strike a balance between these two extremes by seeking a legal entity in which power cannot be confiscated by a few; in which employees, readers, and crowdfunders are guaranteed a say in management; yet in which those who invest more money or effort in the firm command some degree of enhanced voting rights.

A New Model: The NMO

The new model I propose in this book, which I call the Nonprofit Media Organization (NMO), is a hybrid model. It is inspired in part by the model of the great international universities, which combine commercial and noncommercial activities. But there is more to it than that. One goal is to secure permanent financing for the media by freezing their capital. A second goal is to limit the decision-making power of outside shareholders with constraining bylaws.

In a joint-stock company, the issuance of new shares raises two problems. First, the capital of existing shareholders is diluted so that their share of profits decreases, as does the value of their shares should they wish to sell. In the NMO model, this risk does not exist: as a nonprofit corporation, it pays no dividends, and shareholders cannot recover their investments (as in the case of a foundation).

Second, the voting power of existing shareholders is reduced: in other words, their "political" power can evaporate. With a foundation, such a risk does not exist: investors are merely donors and do not acquire voting rights in the governance structure. No matter how large the outside contribution, the incumbent board of directors has all the scope it needs to maintain its power. In the NMO model, the problem of dilution of political power is resolved in a different, more democratic manner: the voting rights of existing shareholders are protected, but some additional power is granted to small contributors, who are regarded as participants in the management of the firm and not mere donors.

The power of money is the principal risk the media face today. As losses mount, media companies have seen their reserves evaporate and have been forced to seek new capital, but under the current system recapitalization carries a heavy price—namely, loss of control.

Any firm needs capital to set itself up in business. The capital supplied by initial investors can be supplemented later by retained profits. Losses, on the other hand, decrease the firm's capital reserves. The initial investors receive shares in the firm as compensation for their investments, and these shares confer certain rights: voting rights, a right to a share of the firm's profits, and a right to sell one's shares at a later date. Hence, power over the firm belongs to those who control its capital: the number of votes accorded to each shareholder is proportional to the number of shares owned.

Now, suppose the firm runs into financial difficulties and is forced to seek additional capital from a new investor. This happened to the French newspaper *Libération* in 2014. Normally, there are two phases to the process. First, operating losses on the firm's balance sheet reduce the value of each share in the company. Indeed, the firm's capital may be entirely wiped out, reducing the share value to zero. New shares are then issued, at which point the new partner may take control of the firm. In 2010, when the Le Monde Group was bought out by investors Pierre Bergé, Xavier Niel, and Matthieu Pigasse, the proportion of shares owned by *Le Monde*'s Society of Journalists, which had been the principal shareholder since 1951, decreased significantly.

Some companies protect themselves against such dilution of ownership and consequent loss of political power by the initial investors by requiring that any change in the firm's capital structure must be approved by a qualified majority at a special shareholders' meeting. But the bylaws of other firms allow new investors to be brought in without prior approval by existing shareholders. This is procedurally simpler but obviously offers no protection against seizure of control by outside investors. It is easier to take control of a firm whose shares are sold publicly on a stock exchange, although as the example of the *New York Times* shows, it is always possible to issue different classes of shares, some of which carry elevated voting rights, in order to limit the effects of a dilution of capital on the control of the firm. For instance, when the *Milwaukee Journal Sentinel,* previously owned by its employees, went public in 2002, employee-held shares were accorded ten votes each compared with one vote for other shares. When Google went public, founders Sergey Brin and Larry Page awarded themselves shares with ten times the voting power of other shares, which enabled them to maintain control of the firm despite becoming minority shareholders.

IN CONTRAST, when a foundation receives a gift, the donor does not acquire any control rights. Many international universities have adopted this model, as have cultural institutions such as museums. A donor may contribute hundreds of millions of euros or dollars without obtaining any voting rights.

Although a few media companies have also adopted this model, it is not ideally suited to the nature of their activities. For example, some readers have contributed money to support their suffering newspapers as if they were forming societies of readers without becoming voting shareholders. The company does not cede any control in exchange for these gifts, so there is no reason to limit their amount. The problem with this model is that it diminishes the incentive for readers (or crowdfunders) to invest, because they get no voice in how the paper is run and must leave all power to the existing shareholders.

Capital and Power

The NMO model I am proposing falls between these two extremes. Like a foundation, it can accept unlimited gifts. Any physical or moral person can contribute. In my model, such gifts are to be tax deductible, as gifts to foundations currently are. Yet they are also to be compensated by voting rights in the firm: a gift to an NMO is a contribution to its capital and therefore brings "political" rights like any other investment.

More precisely, any person contributing more than 1 percent of the capital of an NMO should receive voting rights. (Obviously, the threshold level is open to discussion: it might be set at 0.5 percent or 2 percent instead of 1 percent.) The important point is that individuals contributing less than 1 percent—

crowdfunders, say, or employees of the firm—can form an association for the purpose of obtaining preferential voting rights. To simplify the discussion, I will apply the term *shareholder* to anyone who contributes to the capital of an NMO, even if said shareholder has no right to any dividend and is not allowed to sell his or her shares.

To give an idea of the orders of magnitude involved, the capital of a typical newspaper varies from tens of thousands of euros or dollars for the smallest local dailies (many of which are owned by large media conglomerates) and pure Internet players to hundreds of millions for major national dailies and weekly news magazines. That is why it is important to allow moral persons such as societies of readers to become investors in the larger media companies (because no ordinary reader would be able to meet the 1 percent threshold requirement of such a large company).

Yet—and this is a major feature of the new model I am proposing—these potentially very large investments occur without the risk of a loss of control that exists with an ordinary joint-stock company. How can this be? The key requirement of an NMO is that the rule of proportionality—one share equals one vote—must be set aside.

Voting Rights in NMOs

Concretely, the law could specify, for example, that any investment above, say, 10 percent of the capital of an NMO would bring a less than proportional share of voting rights. For example, investments above the threshold might yield only one-third of a vote per share. Conversely, small investors, who contribute less than 10 percent of the company's capital, would receive a proportionate boost in their voting rights so that the total is always 100 percent.

The coefficient of increase to be applied to small shareholders would depend on the overall structure of capital and could be on the order of 2 or 3, as the examples below illustrate. The crucial point is that individual readers, employees, and crowdfunders who invest less than 1 percent of the firm's capital can join together in one or more associations. For example, there might be an association of readers or friends of the publication and another association of employees.

Crucially, these associations must benefit from the increased voting power accorded to small shareholders even if their combined contribution exceeds 10 percent of the firm's capital. The idea is to give small investors an incentive to invest in order to increase their number. In practice, the law might allow a certain flexibility in setting the key parameters (the 10 percent threshold, the decreased voting rights coefficient of one-third, and the 1 percent threshold) depending on the total capitalization of the firm.[17]

Why would the biggest shareholders choose to invest beyond the threshold at which their voting rights cease to increase as rapidly as the size of their investment? An optimist might say that these generous donors, to borrow Beuve-Méry's formulation, would benefit from demonstrating "the purity of their intentions" and thus "place themselves beyond all suspicion." A more realistic response would be that they would respond to the incentive of tax breaks. The tax benefits would in effect compensate for the decreased voting rights available to large investors.

Note, moreover, that US tax laws already limit the power of major donors to foundations or, more precisely, institute a similar trade-off between power and tax benefits. There are in fact two sorts of nonprofit foundations in the United States: private foundations and public charities. Public charities derive most of their revenue from the general public and receive contributions from a variety of donors: individuals, government, and private foundations. Concretely, at least one-third of contributions must come from donors contributing less than 2 percent of the total contributions. In contrast, private foundations derive most of their resources from a small number of large donors (often an individual, a family, or a firm) and do not solicit funds from the general public. Public charities enjoy a much more favorable tax situation than private foundations.

Illustration

Consider a new NMO that seeks to amass the capital it needs to set itself up in business. For concreteness, let us suppose it is a medium-sized firm (with about forty employees) that estimates it will need a capital of 2.2 million euros to begin operations. The two founders of the company invest 400,000 each, leaving an additional 1.4 million to be raised from other sources.

If this were a traditional joint-stock company, the firm might try to raise 1 million euros from an investment fund, another 5,000 euros from each of its forty employees, and a further 200,000 euros from a crowdsourcing site (2,000 contributions of 100 euros each). This would meet the company's capital needs, but how would voting power be distributed? As we will soon see, the NMO model allows for a much more democratic distribution of power, which makes it a more attractive investment for employees and crowdfunders than the traditional joint-stock company.

In the traditional joint-stock company, the two founders would each have 20 percent of the voting rights, the investment fund 50 percent, and each employee 0.25 percent (or 10 percent for the forty employees together). The small individual donors would have no voice at all. And the investment fund could choose to sell its shares at any moment, thus leaving the firm vulnerable.

What would happen under my NMO model? First, the forty employees could form a society of employees. Similarly, the small individual donors, who would have no voting rights at all in the traditional model, would organize a society of readers. Under the rules described earlier, with a threshold of 10 percent and a coefficient of decrease of one-third for voting rights beyond that threshold, the two groups of crowd-funders would together command nearly 32 percent of the voting rights (16 percent each for readers and employees) and thus a significant share of decision-making power.

The advantages of the NMO model do not end there, however. Since small shareholders play a larger role in the governance of the firm and enjoy better tax advantages, they have a greater incentive to invest. Suppose the real cost to an employee of a 15,000 euro investment is only 5,000 euros, owing to tax benefits. In that case, each employee might choose to invest 15,000 euros, or 400,000 additional euros in all. Donors already enjoy such tax breaks under the current system, but it is reasonable to assume that the further incentive of voting rights would attract a larger number of readers as crowdfunders, raising an additional 600,000 euros (6,000 contributions of 100 euros each).

The founders would then be able to amass the necessary capital without bringing in the investment fund, which in any case may not have been very keen to invest a million euros in a nonprofit venture. And they would be spared the need to cope with the fund's abrupt withdrawal several years down the road. Under the NMO model, the two founders would each hold 14 percent of the voting rights, the society of employees would hold 31 percent, and the society of readers 41 percent. Thus, the balance of power within the firm would be entirely different.

In the current media landscape, it is not hard to find examples of firms that would be able to overcome the crisis if they adopted the NMO model.

The Advantages of the NMO Model

A major advantage of the NMO model is that it allows readers and employees to participate in the firm as crowdfunders and to exercise a voice in its management. Readers and employees obtain voting rights and act as true shareholders. Whereas traditional societies of readers and journalists have not fared well, societies of the new type I envision should be able to play a durable role in the management of NMOs. Why? Because the NMO model affords them a far better legal standing to resist encroachment by outside investors, in contrast to what has happened in numerous instances in recent decades.

The first society of journalists was formed in France in 1951, when a crisis at *Le Monde* led to a transfer of 29 percent of the paper's capital to a society created by its journalists. Subsequently, similar societies were created at a number of publications (including *Le Figaro*, *L'Alsace*, *Les Échos*, and *Ouest-France*). In 1968, the Le Monde Society of Journalists raised its share of the company's capital to 40 percent. But a series of subsequent recapitalizations gradually diluted the society's share to its current level of 5 percent.

In 1973, when *Libération* was founded, the paper's employees owned all of its capital. Little by little, however, majority control slipped out of the hands of employees and into those of outside investors so that today the employee interest is less than 1 percent.

At most other papers, societies of journalists have either ceased to exist or lost their importance. Was this inevitable? Successive recapitalizations were no doubt needed to cover losses or make necessary investments. But was it just or inevitable for the journalists to lose all power over the management of their papers? It was inevitable under the rules of the traditional joint-stock company, but it would not be under the rules of the new NMO.

Under the rules governing joint-stock companies, a recapitalization often involves cancellation of existing shares as losses are written off. In contrast, since there is no sharing of profits in an NMO (and no payment of dividends), losses are not imputed to capital.

Furthermore, any increase of capital automatically results in dilution of the voting rights of existing shareholders. Consider the previous example once again, and suppose that the company's investment requirements oblige it to accept a new investment of 2 million euros. In a joint-stock company, the presence of the new shareholder would decrease the two founders' share of voting rights from 20 to 10 percent, and the combined share of the forty employees would decrease to 5 percent. If the employees wanted to retain their 10 percent collective share, each would have to invest an additional 5,500 euros.

Now consider the case of an NMO (and to simplify the comparison, let us ignore for now the society of readers). With the addition of the new shareholder, each of the forty members of the society of employees would have to invest 600 euros to maintain their collective 10 percent share of voting rights, for an individual cost of 200 euros (thanks to tax deductions). This represents a savings of 5,300 euros per employee. If the employees nevertheless decided to invest the same 5,500 euros each as in the joint-stock case, they would acquire more than 28 percent of the voting rights (after allowing for the tax deduction).

The NMO model thus seeks to limit the omnipotence of very large shareholders. It also provides a lever that small and medium shareholders can use to meet the challenges their organization is facing. It bears emphasizing, however, that the NMO model rejects the notion that there should be absolute and rigid equality among employees (one employee, one vote). It is no use ignoring the importance of capital, which all media organizations need to operate and to invest in new equipment.

Why did societies of journalists fail? Because they tried, like other cooperatives, to give an equal voice to each journalist, regardless of investment in the company. This was an inefficient redistribution of power. In an NMO, voting rights increase with size of contribution up to a certain limit, and if they are reduced beyond that limit, it is in order to give small shareholders an incentive to invest.

In the previous example, it is easy to imagine small investors investing sums of around 50,000 euros. They would then own more than 1 percent of the firm's capital, and their voting rights would be augmented. The NMO thus offers more democracy while acknowledging that democracy in a firm requires capital investments that cannot always be strictly egalitarian.

Another goal of the NMO model is to introduce more democracy by offering tax (and democratic) incentives to organize societies of readers: the news can thus be reappropriated not only by those who produce it but also by those who consume it. Crowdfunding also enhances democracy by granting voting rights to large numbers of small donors, who collectively become not mere donors but full-fledged shareholders. Although they receive no financial compensation, they do obtain a voice in setting the firm's overall direction and key decisions.

An Alternative to Press Subsidies

The NMO model is thus offered as an alternative to the existing system of press subsidies in countries like France, where, as noted, the system suffers both from its complexity and from the arbitrariness of certain decisions (which are left to the discretion of the bureaucracy and media professionals). In countries like the United States, where existing media subsidies are insufficient, it could also provide a novel and extremely efficient way for the government to increase its contribution to the health of the media.

The NMO model offers numerous advantages. It combines the benefits of the nonprofit model with democratized governance, bringing in more small shareholders while also allowing for the large investments that are often needed. Big investors give up some of their decision-making power but in return receive millions in tax breaks. Tax relief in exchange for democratization and capital stabilization: this system resolves the inherent contradictions involved in giving subsidies to media owned by large profit-making corporations or in allowing the press to be controlled by individuals with deep pockets.

In addition, the NMO model offers the advantage of transparency. The tax breaks awarded to donors will automatically and transparently benefit all news media: not only the print press but also the pure Internet players and other innovative new media that may arise in the future. The same tax breaks will apply to all authentic producers of news for the general public, including radio and television, as long as they produce original information. News aggregators, which simply sort and filter news produced by others, will be excluded.

How much will all this cost? That will depend first on the number of firms that choose to organize as NMOs and second on the parameters set by lawmakers (including relevant thresholds and tax exemptions), which will no doubt vary from country to country.[18] Only legislators can determine what tax breaks are appropriate for NMOs. Legislators must also decide what limits, if any, to place on the percentage of NMO revenue that may be derived from advertising.

My purpose here is not to foreclose debate by providing ready-made solutions but to open discussion by suggesting new avenues to explore in the hope of strengthening the media on which our democratic ideals rest.

CONCLUSION

Capitalism and Democracy

IN SOME RESPECTS the crisis of the print media was no doubt inevitable. One can bemoan this fact, bury one's head in the sand, and wait to see what happens. One can quietly wait to die, or one can squarely face the future, take risks, and loudly and clearly proclaim that the media can and must be saved.

Replacing the Stagecoach

What will the future look like? Vice Media or the *New York Times*? ProPublica or the *Washington Post*? BuzzFeed or *USA Today*? Mediapart or *Le Monde*? MailOnline or the Huffington Post? As the economist Joseph Schumpeter pointed out, the railroads were not built by people who owned stagecoaches. In other words, no one should expect tomorrow's revolutions to be led by today's traditional economic actors.

Nevertheless, some newspapers have chosen the path of modernization. They made the jump to the digital world and are shaping the future of the media alongside more recent entrants. Their strategies are diverse and sometimes surprising.

The issue is not to pick winners and losers. Some media outlets will disappear, and we must accept that, even if each loss is heartbreaking. But others will emerge and that should be heartening. The real issue is to continue to produce free, high-quality, unbiased information in a variety of forms and to ensure that it is accessible to all who want it despite dwindling ad revenue and increased competition in a media sector that can support only a limited number of players (of all formats).

The solution I am proposing here—a new legal entity that I call a nonprofit NMO—may seem radical. But it is not all or nothing. Drastic simplification of the existing system of press subsidies in France, a more accommodating legal and fiscal framework for the media in the United States, extension of the VAT reduction to online newspapers in Europe (where the tax break is currently available only to print newspapers), and, more generally, granting media companies everywhere easier access to foundation status and the benefits of private contributions—all of these measures would help. What must be recognized is that the news media provide a public good, just as universities and other contributors to the knowledge economy of the twenty-first century do. For that reason they deserve special treatment by the government.

Endgame?

"Is it over? Are we coming to the end? Will it soon be over?" Governments around the world seem paralyzed by the magnitude of the crisis. If they intervene to help the media, there is a risk that they will be accused of "capturing" their clients. Hence, they hesitate. Despite this risk the French government has created new press subsidies whose allocation appears to be considerably more discretionary than earlier forms of assistance.

Governments have moved gradually toward allowing media companies to operate as nonprofits and therefore to solicit donations. At the same time, they have made it too difficult to acquire nonprofit status because they have not fully embraced the idea that news is a public good. Yet as time goes by, more and more newspapers are shutting down, participation in elections is decreasing everywhere, extremist parties are gaining ground, and political debate is increasingly stultified. The legal and fiscal privileges that other knowledge economy actors (such as universities and research centers) have rightly enjoyed for years are mostly unavailable to the media, to the detriment of the public welfare and democratic ideals.

Hence, we must develop a new, more flexible legal framework for the media: the NMO model I am proposing combines aspects of the foundation and the joint-stock company. It offers new means of financing the media and new ways to share and transmit power. In the current media landscape, it is not difficult to find any number of troubled organizations that could be saved if they adopted the NMO model.

In France, for example, the NMO model would have allowed the employees of the regional daily *Nice-Matin* (then in receivership) to buy the paper without having to cede ownership of *Corse-Matin* or delegate management of the paper to others (as was done under court order in November 2014). If the national daily *Libération* had been an NMO, a third of the staff would not have been forced to leave in early 2015 because of problems linked to the estate of press baron Carlo Caracciolo. Since investments in an NMO are irrevocable, Caracciolo's heirs would not have been able to sell their shares and thus jeopardize the entire system by transferring control to outside investors with little interest in quality news.

In the United States, how many layoffs of journalists might have been avoided if their employers had been NMOs of the type I am proposing? How many newspapers might have been bought out rather than forced to close? The *Milwaukee Journal Sentinel,* which until the early 2000s was owned by its employees, might have chosen to become an NMO rather than go public. It could then have attracted needed financial support from its readers devoted to the widely acknowledged quality of its investigative journalism, as well as from its employees, who would have received tax breaks in exchange for their investments rather than being forced to watch as the value of their shares plummeted on the stock exchange. In view of the steep decline of the paper's stock price in recent years—with dire consequences for its journalists, ranging from salary cuts to early retirement to layoffs—one cannot help thinking that reorganization as an NMO would have been a better solution. This is especially true since the purchase of the paper by the E. W. Scripps Company in 2015, coupled with the spinoff of the profitable audiovisual business that had long subsidized the news operation, suggests that there will soon be additional layoffs and perhaps eventually a shutdown or, at any rate, an end to the print edition. Scripps has already shut down other papers it has purchased, such as the *Cincinnati Post,* the *Albuquerque Tribune,* and the *Rocky Mountain News.* The *Omaha World-Herald* is another venerable American daily that has been publishing for nearly 180 years. Like the *Milwaukee Journal Sentinel,* it was owned by its employees, and its circulation figures suggest that its readers were equally devoted. Both readers and employees would probably have benefited if the paper had adopted the new NMO model I am proposing rather than allowing itself to become another one of Warren Buffet's newspaper assets.

The NMO model would also encourage the creation of new newspapers and online news sites. Under the new model, they would find it easy to raise funds from their readers while at the same time soliciting investments from outside investors without fear of losing control (because the voting rights of those large outside investors would be limited). Existing nonprofit media outlets would also be able to expand. These suffer at present from understaffing due to budgetary limitations, which could be alleviated through crowdsourcing.

Indeed, the NMO model need not be limited to the media. It points to the need for a new legal entity between the foundation and the joint-stock company as well as to the importance of rethinking the way in which power is shared under capitalism so as to make it more democratic. We need to find a middle ground between the illusion of hypercooperation (one person, one vote) and hypercapitalism (in which large investors wield unlimited power). The model also suggests ways to smooth the transfer of power between generations and to involve wider circles of people in company decisions.

The media are particularly ripe for adoption of this new model. The difficulties they face are such that there is no time for delay. A choice has to be made. New technologies such as the Internet have opened the way to a democratization of capitalism, of which crowdfunding is one sign. But pure gifts are not enough: contributors should receive voting rights and political power as incentives to invest and as a means to reassert control over our collective destiny. Capitalism, crowdfunding, democracy: these are watchwords for the future.

NOTES

This book is supplemented by an online technical appendix, where interested readers will find a detailed presentation of the sources and methods used in the work as well as a sample media corporation charter. There is also a media corporation simulator along with detailed descriptions of the various media companies and groups mentioned in the text. See www.sites.google.com/site/juliacagehomepage/sauver-les-medias.

Introduction

1. In addition, the site Paper Cuts (www.newspaperlayoffs.com) reports on layoffs, which number in the hundreds.

2. See André Schiffrin, *L'Argent et les Mots* (Paris: La Fabrique, 2010); and Robert McChesney and John Nichols, *The Death and Life of Great American Newspapers* (Philadelphia: Nation Book, 2010).

3. Matthew Gentzkow, Edward L. Glaeser, and Claudia Goldin illustrate the corruption of American newspapers in the 1870s by recounting

the press coverage of the Crédit Mobilier scandal in "The Rise of the Fourth Estate: How Newspapers Became Informative and Why It Mattered," in *Corruption and Reform: Lessons from America's Economic History* (Cambridge, MA: National Bureau of Economic Research, 2006).

4. The "society of readers" and "society of journalists" are specifically French phenomena that first emerged in the second half of the twentieth century. The first society of journalists was created in 1951 at the newspaper *Le Monde.* The paper's journalists formed a society that acquired 28.57 percent of the paper's capital. I describe these societies—and their limits—in more detail in Chapter 3.

5. In a number of countries, including the United States, Austria, and Belgium, state aid for newspapers mainly takes the form of indirect government support, such as favorable postal rates and tax breaks. In France the government has also introduced a number of direct government subsidy schemes for newspapers. These schemes are described in more detail in Chapter 2.

1. The Information Age?

1. *L'Apport de la culture à l'économie en France,* a report by the Inspection Générale des Finances and the

Inspection Générale des Affaires Culturelles, December 2013.

2. These figures are estimates by the French Bureau of Economic Analysis (BEA) and the US National Endowment for the Arts (NEA) for 2011. Artistic and cultural production in the United States were hit particularly hard by the recession of 2007–2009: they accounted for 3.6 percent of GDP before the crisis and as much as 3.7 percent in 2004.

3. This figure comes from the Department for Culture, Media and Sport, "Creative Industries Economic Estimates. January 2014. Statistical Release," available at www.gov.uk. The cultural contribution to GDP has risen sharply in recent years, from 4.7 percent in 2008 to 5.2 percent in 2012.

4. The figure for higher education (1.5 percent) is slightly less than the Organisation for Economic Co-operation and Development (OECD) average (1.6 percent). See *Education at a Glance 2013: OECD Indicators* (Paris: OECD Publishing, 2013).

5. See, especially, Pierre Rosanvallon, *Counter-Democracy: Politics in an Age of Mistrust*, trans. Arthur Goldhammer (Cambridge: Cambridge University Press, 2008); and *Democratic Legitimacy: Impartiality, Reflexivity, Proximity,*

trans. Arthur Goldhammer (Princeton, NJ: Princeton University Press, 2011).

6. "The President's Budget for Fiscal Year 2016": http://www.gpo.gov/fdsys/pkg/BUDGET-2016 -BUD/pdf/BUDGET-2016-BUD.pdf.

7. The category "management and higher intellectual professions" was not defined in France prior to the 1954 census.

8. See Alex Jones, *Losing the News* (Oxford: Oxford University Press, 2010); and Éric Scherer, *A-t-on encore besoin de journalistes? Manifeste pour un "journalisme augmenté"* (Paris: PUF, 2011).

9. See Figure A.1 in the online technical appendix.

10. The two pages can be compared in the online appendix.

11. The page size was reduced by roughly 11 percent, but this was partly compensated by an increase in page count. See Katharine Q. Seelye, "*Times* to Reduce Page Size and Close a Plant in 2008," *New York Times,* July 18, 2006.

12. On online publishing practices, see Julia Cagé, Nicolas Hervé, and Marie-Luce Viaud, "The Production of Information in an Online World," Sciences Po Paris Working Paper, 2015: http:// econ.sciences-po.fr/sciences-po-economics -discussion-papers. Also available at: https://sites .google.com/site/juliacagehomepage/research.

13. Mario Vargas Llosa, *La tia Julia y el escribidor* (Barcelona: Seix Barral, 1977).

14. Quoted in Ignacio Ramonet, *L'Explosion du journalisme: Des médias de masse à la masse des médias* (Paris: Galilée, 2011).

2. The End of Illusions

1. See, for example, André Schiffrin, *L'Argent et les Mots;* Marc Martin, *Trois siècles de publicité en France* (Paris: Odile Jacob, 1992); and Patrick Eveno, *Les médias sont-ils sous influence?* (Paris: Larousse, 2008).

2. Patrick Eveno, *Histoire de la presse française: De Théophraste Renaudot à la révolution numérique* (Paris: Flammarion, 2012).

3. Michael Schudson, *Discovering the News: A Social History of American Newspapers* (London: Basic Books, 1981).

4. The online appendix includes data for Austria, Belgium, Canada, Denmark, Finland, Italy, Japan, the Netherlands, and Sweden. All data are taken from the ADSPEND database of the World Advertising Research Center (WARC).

5. See Figures A.2 to A.10 in the online technical appendix.

6. For a broad overview, see Sylvain Parasie, *Et maintenant, une page de pub: Une histoire morale de la*

publicité à la télévision française (Paris: INA
Éditions, 2010).

7. Charles Angelucci and Julia Cagé, "Newspapers
in Times of Low Advertising Revenues," Sciences
Po Working Paper, 2014.

8. See Figure A.11 in the online technical appendix.

9. "Storytelling Ads May Be Journalism's New
Peril," in the *New York Times,* September 15, 2013.

10. According to data compiled by the Pew Research
Center.

11. To be more precise, in the newspaper business,
some costs, such as the costs of paper, printing,
and delivery, increase with demand. This is not
the case with television or radio. If the web won
out entirely over the print media, the costs
associated with increasing market size would
disappear.

12. When will we see Jean Seberg hawking *Le Monde
International* on Fifth Avenue? The *New York Times*
was able to export its brand, but *Le Monde* has
unfortunately been unable thus far to exploit
its prestige to penetrate the fledgling print
market in Francophone Africa.

13. In France, as Patrick Eveno points out, Charles-
Joseph Panckoucke, the publisher of the *Encylo-
pédie,* owned, in the era of the French Revolution,
La Gazette, Le Moniteur, and *Le Mercure de France.*
After Hachette's "green octopus," Robert Hersant

built a press empire in France, and today there is Michel Lucas, the president of Crédit Mutuel, who owns EBRA (Est Bourgogne Rhône Alpes), the largest regional press group in France (*L'Est républicain, L'Alsace, Le Dauphiné libéré,* etc.). This is partly due to economies of scale in an industry with high fixed costs.

14. Eli Noam, *Media Ownership and Concentration in America* (Oxford: Oxford University Press, 2009).

15. Note, however, that American law is evolving in this regard. The Federal Communications Commission (FCC) has attempted on several occasions since 2002 to weaken restrictions on media ownership, thus far in vain. But certain de facto instances of cross-ownership exist. In France, the Socialist Party promised in 2011 to update the law on media control, but it has yet to do so.

16. Matthew Gentzkow and Jesse Shapiro, "Competition and Truth in the Market for News," *Journal of Economic Perspectives,* 22(2), 2008, pp. 133–154.

17. Timothy Besley and Andrea Prat, "Handcuffs for the Grabbing Hand? Media Capture and Government Accountability," *American Economic Review,* 96(3), 2006, pp. 720–736.

18. The "age of giants" borrows from the title of Dennis F. Herrick's *Media Management in the Age of Giants: Business Dynamics of Journalism,* 2nd ed.

(Albuquerque: University of New Mexico Press, 2012).

19. See Julia Cagé, "Media Competition, Information Provision and Political Participation," Working Paper, Harvard and Paris, Harvard University and Sciences Po Paris, 2014.

20. Is this changing? *Times* advertisers have just agreed to pay the same price for a print ad as for an ad in the paper's tablet app. But reader attention time is roughly similar for print and for the tablet app, whereas it is much lower for the general web reader, and websites' ads remain cheaper.

21. See www.niemanlab.org/2014/07/when-a-digital -subscription-costs-more-than-a-print-one.

22. On press subsidies in France, see Julia Cagé and Etienne Fize, "The Effectiveness of Public Support to the Press: Evidence from France," Sciences Po Paris Working Paper, 2015. For a global overview of press subsidies in fifteen countries from Australia and Bulgaria to Finland and the United States, see Paul Murschetz, ed., *State Aid for Newspapers: Theories, Cases, Actions* (Berlin: Springer, 2013). The examples studied in this section are drawn mainly from these two sources.

23. In 1973, with certain low-circulation papers facing growing difficulties, the French govern-

ment decided to grant them additional aid, effectively ending the system of neutral subsidies. Similarly, Austria introduced direct subsidies of newspapers in 1975, as did Belgium in 1973 (but these were gradually eliminated after 1997).

24. Including Germany, Austria, Belgium, Denmark, Finland, France, Ireland, Italy, the Netherlands, Norway, the United Kingdom, Sweden, and Switzerland.

25. Similarly, in 1985 Austria introduced a "special subsidy for the maintenance of variety" to support minor newspapers.

26. Baines, "United Kingdom: Subsidies and Democratic Deficits in Local News," in *State Aid for Newspapers,* ed. Paul C. Murschetz (Berlin: Springer, 2013).

27. Inspection Générale des Finances and the Inspection Générale des Affaires Culturelle, *L'Apport de la culture à l'économie en France.*

28. Centre National du Cinéma et de l'Image Animée, "Soutien au cinéma, à l'audiovisuel et au multimédia: Rapport et Perspectives, 2013–2015." http://www.cnc.fr/c/document_library/get _file?uuid=c9f5aa7c-5a5a-4ca0-8f8e -6e1c49fc5b63&groupId=18.

29. The "film tax relief" totaled 220 million pounds according to HM Revenue and Customs.

30. BBC Annual Report and Accounts, 2013–2014. https://www.gov.uk/government/uploads/system /uploads/attachment_data/file/342211/bbc _annualreport_201314.pdf.

31. Corporation for Public Broadcasting, "Appro-priation Request and Justification. FY2015 and FY2017," March 5, 2014. Whether or not as a result of this low level of public financing, the audience for public radio and television is extremely small in the United States by inter-national standards. http://www.cpb.org. /appropriation/justification-FY15-and-FY17.pdf

32. According to a report prepared by deputy Michel Françaix, "Médias, livre et industries culturelles: Presse," October 2012. http://www.assemblee -nationale.fr/14/pdf/budget/plf2013/a0252-tVI.pdf.

33. Nichols, *Death and Life of Great American Newspapers.*

34. Lee C. Bollinger, *Uninhibited, Robust, and Wide-Open: A Free Press for a New Century* (Oxford: Oxford University Press, 2010).

35. The Supreme Court abolished these limits with its ruling in *McCutcheon v. FEC* on April 2, 2014. An individual may now contribute up to $3.47 million per election cycle. On the Supreme Court and campaign financing in the United States, see Robert C. Post, *Citizens Divided* (Cambridge, MA: Harvard University Press, 2014).

36. See Timothy K. Kuhner, *Capitalism v. Democracy: Money in Politics and the Free Market Constitution* (Stanford, CA: Stanford Law Books, 2014); and Lawrence Lessig, *Republic, Lost: How Money Corrupts Congress—and a Plan to Stop It* (New York: Twelve/Hachette Book Group, 2011).

37. Adam Bonica, Nolan McCarty, Keith T. Poole, and Howard Rosenthal, "Why Hasn't Democracy Slowed Rising Inequality?" *Journal of Economic Perspectives,* 27(3), 2013, pp. 103–124.

38. Martin Gilens, *Affluence and Influence: Economic Inequality and Political Power in America* (Princeton, NJ: Princeton University Press, 2012). See also Martin Gilens and Benjamin I. Page, "Testing Theories of American Politics: Elites, Interest Groups, and Average Citizens," *Perspective on Politics,* 12(3), pp. 564–581. And for a comparative approach, see Larry M. Bartels, "The Social Welfare Deficit: Public Opinion, Policy Responsiveness, and Political Inequality in Affluent Democracies," Vanderbilt University Working Paper, 2015.

3. A New Model for the Twenty-First Century

1. James O'Shea, *The Deal from Hell: How Moguls and Wall Street Plundered Great American Newspapers* (New York: PublicAffairs, 2011).

2. Gilbert Cranberg, Randall P. Bezanson, and John Soloski, *Taking Stock: Journalism and the Publicly Traded Newspaper Company* (Mississauga: Wiley, 2001).

3. O'Shea, *Deal from Hell.*

4. A recent report by the FCC points out the crying lack of local news in many American communities. See FCC, "The Information Needs of Community: The Changing Media Landscape in a Broadband Age," 2011. https://transition.fcc .gov/osp/inc-report/The_Information_Needs_of _Communities.pdf.

5. Markus Prior, *Post-Broadcast Democracy: How Media Choice Increases Inequality in Political Involvement and Polarizes Elections* (Cambridge: Cambridge University Press, 2007).

6. As the parent company of the group RTL, Bertelsmann has a presence in French radio (RTL, RTL2, Fun Radio) and television (M6). Through its share of Prisma Media, it is also involved in the press *(Capital, VSD, Voici, Gala, Télé Loisirs).*

7. Just as gifts to foundations are irrevocable. Note, however, that while the investment is irrevocable, the NMO is nevertheless authorized to spend it.

8. The association that owns the company that runs *Ouest-France* guarantees the newspaper's

independence because no one can become
a member of the organization without the
approval of the board of directors.

9. The nonprofit sector is strictly defined by
Section 501(c)3 of the US tax code. A nonprofit organization must reinvest all of its
earnings and may not pay dividends. Individual
contributions may be deducted from federal
income tax, and the organization itself is
exempt from certain federal taxes. To meet
the requirements of Section 501(c)3, an NMO
must demonstrate that it serves an educational
need.

10. See the Pew Research Center study "Nonprofit
Journalism: A Growing But Fragile Part of the
U.S. News System," June 2013, www.journalism
.org/2013/06/10/nonprofit-journalism/, as well
as the Knight Foundation report "Finding a
Foothold: How Nonprofit News Ventures Seek
Sustainability," 2013, www.knightfoundation
.org/features/nonprofitnews/.

11. Robert W. McChesney and Victor Pickard, eds.,
*Will the Last Reporter Please Turn Out the Lights?
The Collapse of Journalism and What Can Be Done to
Fix It* (New York: The New Press, 2011). As an
alternative to Section 501(c)3, Leonard Downie
Jr. and Michael Schudson propose in *The
Reconstruction of American Journalism,* chap. 5, that

newspapers be chartered as "Low-Profit Limited Liability Corporations" (L3C), a legal hybrid of for- and nonprofit types. www.cjr.org /reconstruction/the_reconstruction_of _american.php in the *Columbia Journalism Review.*

12. The difficulties faced by Haverhill Matters, a website owned by a local news co-op, which has yet to amass adequate funding despite several years of trying, attest to the limits of the cooperative formula in the media sector.

13. On the advantages of the ESOP and its importance in the US economy, see Joseph R. Blasi, Richard B. Freeman, and Douglas L. Kruse, *The Citizen's Share: Putting Ownership Back into Democracy* (New Haven, CT: Yale University Press, 2013).

14. This type of corporate entity was created by a law of 1917. In a *SAPO,* there are two types of shares: standard shares (parts of capital) and so-called work shares, which are awarded to employees as a group by way of a workers' cooperative.

15. In addition to the *Inter-County Leader,* other examples of surviving cooperatives include the *West Highland Free Press* in the United Kingdom and the Media Co-Op in Canada, a network of cooperatives providing participatory local media coverage. In Germany, *Die Tageszeitung (TAZ)* has also adopted a cooperative model: the daily is owned by its readers (nearly 15,000 strong) on

the one person, one vote model regardless of how much capital each has contributed. Anyone can become a member by contributing a sum of 500 to 25,000 euros.

16. See, for example, Michael Kremer, "Why Are Worker Cooperatives So Rare?," National Bureau of Economic Research (NBER) Working Paper no. 6118, 1997, www.nber.org/papers/w6118.

17. All the rules are precisely set forth in the online appendix, in which I indicate the mathematical rule relating the coefficient of increase to the other parameters. The reader will also find a simulator with which to reproduce the examples given below and to generate others at the following website: www.sites.google.com/site/juliacagehomepage /sauver-les-medias.

18. In France today, the tax deduction for donations to nonprofits is currently 66 percent of the amount donated up to a limit of 20 percent of the donor's taxable income. If the 20 percent ceiling is exceeded, the tax deduction can be spread over a five-year period.

INDEX

Advertising revenue, 5, 19, 28, 42–53, 93–94; and readership, 67–68, 93

Agence-France Presse (AFP), 30, 38, 72–73

Aggregation, 2, 14, 38–39, 130

Albuquerque Tribune, 136

Alsace, L', 125

Alternatives économiques, 112

Amazon, 53, 82, 106

American Society of News Editors, 29

Antitrust laws and monopolies, 58–61

Associated Press (AP), 30, 102

Aujourd'hui en France, 77

Australia, newspaper tax breaks, 71

Australian, 57

Baines, David, 72

Balzac, Honoré de, 90

BBC. *See* British Broadcasting Corporation (BBC)

Bergé, Pierre, 116

Berkshire Hathaway, 57, 68, 111

Bertelsmann Foundation and family, 8, 96–99, 150n6

Beuve-Méry, Hubert, 97, 121

Bezos, Jeff, 80, 82

Blair, Jayson, 34

Bollinger, Lee, 80

Boston Globe, 32, 61, 81, 91

Brin, Sergey, 117

British Broadcasting Corporation (BBC), 4–5, 59, 76

British Film Institute (BFI), 76

BSkyB, 58

Buffett, Warren, 57, 136

BuzzFeed, 31, 52, 131

Cable news, 2

Cameron, David, 76

Campaign finance, 84–86, 88

Canada, campaign finance, 84

Caracciolo, Carlo, 87, 134

Cardin, Ben, 105

Carr, David, 52

Center for Investigative Reporting, 103

Centre National du Cinéma et de l'Image Animée (CNC), 75

Chandler, Harry, 83

Charlie Hebdo, 65

Chicago Examiner, 57

Chicago Tribune, 4, 92

Chinatown, 83

Christian Science Monitor, 102

Cincinnati Post, 136

Citizen Kane, 83

Cleveland Plain Dealer, 28

Commission on Professional Journalist Identity Cards (CCIJP), 21

Corporation for Public Broadcasting (CPB), 76

Corse-Matin, 73, 134

Courrier picard, Le, 110, 112

Croix, La, 35, 77

Crowdfunding, 11, 89–90, 104; incentives to invest, 100, 113, 118–119, 125, 128

Daily Telegraph, 31, 43

Dassault Aviation, 106

Denmark: campaign finance, 85; newspaper

tax subsidies and breaks, 72

Dirks, Van Essen & Murray, 7

Dow Jones & Company, 91

Drahi, Patrick, 81

E. W. Scripps, 60, 135–136

East End News, 110

Échos, Les, 77, 125

El Pais, 28

Elections and politics: decrease in regional press, effect of, 63; public companies, effect on, 93

Facebook. *See* Social media

FAZIT-Stiftung, 101

Figaro, Le, 4, 35, 65, 77, 106, 125

First Look Media, 81

Foundations: higher education, 18; media ownership and governance of, 96–99; reform

of laws governing bylaws, 108–109. *See also* Voting rights

Fox News, 57, 86

France: antitrust laws or government monopoly, 58–59; campaign finance, 84; daily regional press, competition in, 62–63; government, taxes to subsidize, 77, 78–79; government support by sector, 75; joint-stock companies model for newspapers, 95; journalists in, 21–24, 28, 142n7; law of 1901 association, 101; legal definition of news, 20, 31; newspaper advertising revenue, 43–47, 52; newspaper tax subsidies and breaks, 70, 72–73, 146n23; nonprofit organization statutes and NMOs, 105, 107–108; reform of laws governing foundation

France *(continued)*
bylaws, 108–109; subsidy reform, 129, 133; television advertising in, 48–49; website visit increase, 65; worker shareholder corporation (*SAPO*), 111; workers' cooperative production societies (*SCOPs*), 110, 112

France Televisions, 4

France-Soir, 3, 7

Frankfurter Allgemeine Zeitung (*FAZ*), 101

Free, 81

Gannett Group, 28, 60, 91

Gawker, 31

Gazette (Cedar Rapids, Iowa), 111

Germany: advertising revenue, 46f–47; Bertelsmann Foundation, 96–98

Gilens, Martin, 86

Girardin, Émile de, 5–6, 44

Google, 2, 38, 53

Governance and financing of media, 8, 10–11; public good and financing, 106; reform of laws governing foundation bylaws, 108–109; subsidies, government, 70–74; subsidies, newswire, 30; taxes and other payments to governments, 77–78; workers' cooperatives, 110–113, 152n12, 152n15. *See also* Voting rights

Government media monopolies, 58–59

Greensboro News and Record, 67

Greenwald, Glenn, 81

Guardian, 8, 56, 101; nonprofit media organization, 101; website, 56

Guardian Media Group, 101

Hearst, William Randolph, 57

Henry, John, 80, 81

Herald Sun, 57

Hersant Group, 7

Huffington Post, 33, 131

Intercept, 81

Inter-County Leader, 111

Internal Revenue Code Section 501(c)3, 104–105, 108, 151n9

International New York Times, 57

International Reporting Project, 96

Internet: effects of, 25–26, 32; nonprofit media organizations and, 103

Irish Times, nonprofit media organization, 101

Journal Communications, 60

Journal Media Group, 60

Journalists: decline in print media employment, 23–29; definition of, 21; foreign correspondents, 33; newspaper staff cuts and layoffs, 28–29, 31, 36, 56, 135; staff size and quality, 56

Kelley, Jack, 34

Knowledge economy, 12–15; government support, 74–78, 107, 134; media sector, 15–16

Koch, Charles and David, 86

La peau de chagrin (Balzac), 90, 92

La Tribune, 3

Lagardère Group, 61

Le Monde Group, 116

Ledoux, Bruno, 69

L'Humanité, 73, 77

Libération, 4, 9, 69, 73, 77, 87; ownership and stock dilution, 81, 116, 125, 134

Los Angeles Times, 4, 35, 83

MailOnline, 131

Manchester, Doug, 81

Mashable, 31

McChesney, Robert, 80

Media General Inc., 7, 57

Media industry, economics of, 4–5; competition, effects of, 61–64; fixed costs and market share, 56–58, 144n11; irrevocable capital endowments proposal, 108; monopoly and consolidation, 56–61, 144n13, 145n15. *See also* Nonprofit media organization (NMO)

Mediapart, 33, 39, 81, 131

Milwaukee Journal Sentinel, 117, 135–136

Mohn family, 97–98

Monde, Le, 10, 39, 73, 77, 144n12; advertising in, 36; ownership, 81, 95, 116, 125; readership, 66; Society of Journalists, 10, 116, 125, 140n4; staff size, 37; supplements, 36; website, 16, 30–31, 65, 66–67

Montagne, La, 101–102

Murdoch, Rupert and family, 57, 60, 86, 98–99

Native advertising, 48, 52–53

New York (Morning) Journal, 57

New York Post, 58

New York Sun, 44

New York Times, 17, 20, 91, 131; native advertising on, 52; page counts and fonts, 35, 142n11; readership, 66, 146n20; revenue, advertising and subscription, 49, 51, 68;

staff size, 37; supplements, 36

New York Times Company, 61, 91; voting rights and class of shares, 117

New York Times website, 53; online views and viewers, 67; paywalls, 69

News: definition of, 19–20, 31; online, 32, 37, 38. *See also* Quality, journalistic

News & Record, 57

News agencies. *See* Agence-France Presse (AFP); Associated Press (AP); Reuters

News Corp, 60

News on Sunday, 111

Newspaper Death Watch, 4

Newspapers: competition, effects of, 61–63; duplication of coverage, 29–30; economic decline and shutdowns, 2–5, 133, 136; ownership and political influence, 82–86; revenue, advertising, 43, 48; revenue, government support, 70–74, 147n24; revenue, trends, 54–55; subscriptions, print and online, 68–69

NextRadioTV, 82

Nice-Matin, 134

Nice-Matin Group, 3

Nichols, John, 80

Niel, Xavier, 81, 116

Noam, Eli, 58

Nonprofit journalism, *Guardian*, 8

Nonprofit media organization (NMO), 89–90, 101; active examples, 101–102; advantages of, 125, 129–130, 136; foundation and joint-stock company model, 10, 100, 109, 114, 129, 134, 136–137; funding and decision-making, 10–11, 100, 104, 109–110, 130, 140n5, 150n7, 153n18; permanent financing of NMOs, 114, 135; statutes

Nonprofit media organ-
ization (NMO) *(continued)*
    governing status,
    104–106, 132–133; tax
    benefits of investing,
    121–122, 124; weak-
    nesses of, 103. *See also*
    Crowdfunding; Voting
    rights
Norway, newspaper tax
    subsidies and breaks, 71,
    73
Nouvel Observateur, Le , 81, 87
*Nouvelle République du
    Centre-Ouest, La*, *(SAPO)*,
    111

Office de Radiodiffusion-
    Télévision Française
    (ORTF), 59
Oklahoma Watch, 96
Omaha World Herald, 57,
    111, 136
Omidyar, Pierre, 80, 81
Orange County Register, 68
O'Reilly, Bill, 34
Osborne, Peter, 43

Otis, Harrison Gray, 83
Ouest-France, 16, 101, 125,
    150n8
Ownership of media:
    diversity of, 9–10, 17;
    family foundations,
    96–99; government
    support of, 76; joint-
    stock companies, 17,
    18–19, 94–95, 99, 106,
    114; nonprofits, 17

Page, Larry, 117
Paid posts. *See* Native
    advertising
Participatory financing.
    See Crowdfunding
Penguin Random House, 96
Perdriel, Claude, 87
Pigasse, Matthieu, 116
Politico, 39, 52–53
Pompidou, Georges, 49
Portland Oregonian, 28
Postal Act of 1792, 71
Postal Reorganization Act
    of 1970, 80
Poynter Institute, 102

Press cards. *See* Commission on Professional Journalist Identity Cards (CCIJP)

Print media. *See* Newspapers

ProPublica, 8, 102, 103, 131

Publicly traded companies, 80–87, 90–92, 94, 117

Pugachev, Alexander, 7

Quality, journalistic, 24–37, 41, 56, 68; American Society of Newspaper Editors, principles of, 95; content repetition, 2, 5–6; effect of public companies, 92, 94; goal of media companies, 90, 94, 132; investigative reporting, 32–33, 81, 102–103, 135

Quartz, 33

Radio France, 4

Reuters, 38

Rocky Mountain News, 136

Roularta Media Group, 81

San Diego Union-Tribune, 81

San Francisco Examiner, 57

Sandler, Herbert and Marion, 8, 102

Scherer, Éric, 32

Schmidt, Eric, 39

Schumpeter, Joseph, 131

SCOP. See under France

Scott Trust, 101

Social media: Facebook, 1, 48, 53; Twitter, 1, 38, 48

Sociétés Coopératives Ouvrières de Production, 9, 110

Society of Journalists, 10, 116, 125, 140n4

Spiegel, Der, 111–112

State Press (Arizona State University), 96

Sud-Ouest, 4

Sun, 58

Sunday Times, 58

Sweden, newspaper tax subsidies and breaks, 71
Sydney Morning Herald, 36

Tampa Bay Times, 102
Texas Tribune, 102
The Hour, 59
Time, Inc., 60
Time Warner, 60
Times, 36, 43, 58
Tribune Company, 29, 60
Tulsa World, 57
21st Century Fox, 60, 98
Twitter. *See* Social media

United Kingdom: BBC monopoly, 59; media industry government support, 75; newspaper tax break on VAT, 71, 72
United States, 52; advertising revenue, 44, 46f–47, 49–51f, 93; antitrust laws, 58–59; campaign finance, 84, 85–86, 148n35; local reporting decline, 33; newspaper tax subsidies and breaks, 71, 74, 76–77, 107–108; newspapers, employment decline, 26–29; quality journalism and publicly held companies, 94–95; state-owned media, 96; subsidy reform, 80, 129; tax-exempt status, 104–105
USA Today, 60, 131

Varenne, Alexander and Marguerite, 102
Vargas Llosa, Mario, 39
Vice Media, 33, 131
Voice of America, 96
Voice of San Diego, 104
Voleur, Le (The Thief), 6
Voting rights: employee loss of, 126; foundations, 91, 98, 114–115, 117; joint-stock companies, 99, 114, 117, 121–122,

126; nonprofit media organization, 100, 115, 118, 119, 120–124, 127–128; ownership and, 9, 10, 117; small shareholders and, 100, 120, 123–124, 128, 129

Vox Media, Chorus for Advertisers, 52–53

Wall Street Journal, 35, 58, 91

Washington Post, 35, 82, 106, 131

Washington Post Company, 91

Websites: effect on newspaper jobs, 30–31;

Google News, 38–39; online news content, 38–39; online newspaper views and viewers, 65–67; paywalls, 69

Whittingdale, John, 76

Williams, Brian, 34

Worker shareholder corporation (société anonyme à participation ouvrière, or *SAPO*), 111, 113, 152n14

Workers' Production Cooperatives, 9

Yahoo News, 39

Yonne républicaine, L', 110, 112